XANDRA BINGLEY rode and trained ponies before she started work
at 17 for MI5. She worked for the *Atlantic Monthly Review* in Boston
and the Kennedy Institute of Politics at Harvard, lived in Ireland and
in London, became a publisher's reader and then a commissioning
editor at Jonathan Cape before starting her own literary agency. She
has a son, a daughter and a grandson, and lives in Primrose Hill.
This is her first book.

Visit www.AuthorTracker.co.uk for exclusive information
on your favourite HarperCollins authors.

From the reviews of *Bertie, May and Mrs Fish*:

'An instant English classic – a book about class, courage, innocence,
survival and the "losts" and "founds" of wartime Britain, written
with such wit, generosity and panache that it's a galloping runaway
pleasure to read'
ALI SMITH

'There is nothing usual about Bingley's story or her way of telling
it. It is full of bright colours like a child's paintbox, and its short,
present-tense sentences capture the unguarded immediacy of childhood experience. It instantly takes its place beside country classics
such as *Lark Rise to Candleford* and *Cider with Rosie*'
JOHN CAREY, *Sunday Times*

'Seemingly artless, this story is in fact told with great technical skill
. . . you would need to have lost touch with all feeling not to be
moved to tears by the book's final chapter. *Bertie, May and Mrs Fish*
has all the makings of a minor classic'
PETER PARKER, *Daily Telegraph*

'Enchanting . . . this evocative bool

D1422316

'Within every landed country family there are skeletons and sorrows, hardships which follow the harrow and unsentimental resignation about life on the land. Seldom has such an account been told with less rancour and more warmth than by Xandra Bingley . . . That she can tell the tale with love and not bitterness . . . is both the lesson and the triumph of her story' *Country Life*

BERTIE, MAY AND MRS FISH

Country Memories of Wartime

Xandra Bingley

HARPER PERENNIAL
London, New York, Toronto and Sydney

Harper Perennial
An imprint of HarperCollins*Publishers*
77–85 Fulham Palace Road
Hammersmith
London w6 8jb

www.harperperennial.co.uk

This edition published by Harper Perennial 2006

1 3 5 7 9 8 6 4 2

First published by HarperCollins*Publishers* 2005

Copyright © Xandra Bingley 2005
PS Section © Xandra Bingley 2006

PS™ is a trademark of HarperCollins*Publishers* Ltd

Xandra Bingley asserts the moral right to be
identified as the author of this work

A catalogue record for this book is
available from the British Library

ISBN-13 978-0-00-714951-3
ISBN-10 0-00-714951-4

Map of Pegglesworth Farm drawn by Rex Nicholls

Illustrations pages 33, 51, 54, 55, 70, 155, 193 © Michael Lyne

All other illustrations © The Estate of Lionel Edwards by courtesy of
Felix Rosenstiel's Widow & Son Limited, London

Set in PostScript Monotype Dante by
Rowland Phototypesetting Ltd, Bury St Edmunds, Suffolk

Printed and bound in Great Britain by
Clays Ltd, St Ives plc

For my grandparents
Elizabeth and Noel Bingley
Eva and Hubert Lenox-Conyngham

Contents

It never harms to exaggerate in the direction of truth.

Henri Matisse, to an art student

Across the snowy hills some galloping horsemen are chasing a single horseman. He is beating his horse and racing away downhill to escape. He reaches flat white land and gallops on and on, looking over his shoulder, beating his horse. The others do not follow him away from the hills.

At last he arrives at a village exhausted and people crowd around him and exclaim, 'You are safe . . . it is wonderful . . . we never believed you would get here.' He says, 'I can tell you I was afraid, they got close to me up in the hills.'

The people say, 'No – no – you do not understand . . . it is a miracle . . . you have ridden across the lake . . . underneath the ice is water a mile deep.'

Then he dies. From fear of a danger he did not know he was in.

German fable

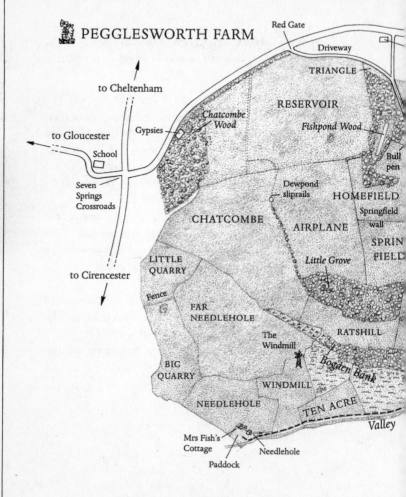

PEGGLESWORTH FARM

Red Gate

Driveway

to Cheltenham

TRIANGLE

RESERVOIR

Chatcombe
Wood

Gypsies

Fishpond Wood

to Gloucester

School

Bull
pen

Seven
Springs
Crossroads

Dewpond
sliprails

HOMEFIELD

Springfield
wall

CHATCOMBE

AIRPLANE

SPRIN
FIELD

LITTLE
QUARRY

Little Grove

to Cirencester

Fence

FAR
NEEDLEHOLE

The
Windmill

RATSHILL

Bogden Bank

BIG
QUARRY

WINDMILL

NEEDLEHOLE

TEN ACRE

Valley

Mrs Fish's
Cottage

Needlehole

Paddock

------------ Mrs Fish's ride from the farm to Needlehole

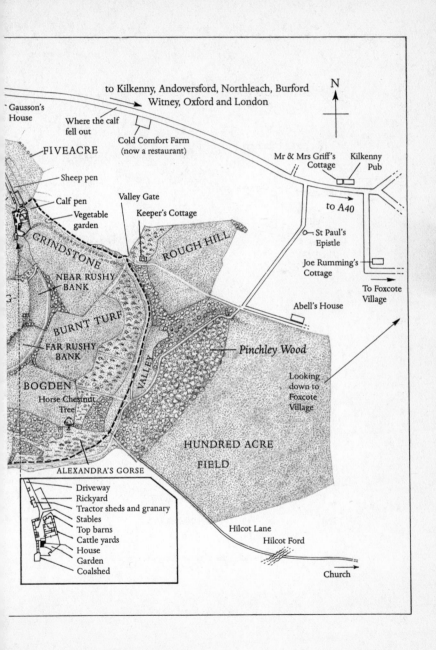

HOMEFIELD

After wartime my father sends home bales of midnight-blue and plum-red velvet for downstairs curtains, a cinecamera and roll-down screen, two black bearskin coats, a touring Bentley and a dinner service for twelve of creamy rippling Copenhagen china hand-painted with wildflowers.

He writes to my mother ... Now we'll have some damned good fun.

And that's what he says when he is home on leave and a thousand daffodil and narcissus bulbs arrive from Holland in plywood boxes. He spills whitewash from a blue speckled tin bucket in a half-moon arc from the coal shed oak to the damson tree by the bridge on the Rushy Brook stream and marks off half an acre of Homefield and shouts . . . Mind out of the way you bloody child . . . as I run over his white line. I am four years old and not afraid.

A post and rails goes up along the marker line. Joe Rummings slams the iron crowbar in the ground. Griff drops spiked ash stakes in the holes and swings an oak mallet. The Ayrshire milking herd chew cud in  Homefield and watch nails hammered into split ash rails.

My father walks about with a box. He swings up one arm and throws a handful of bulbs that spray the pale blue autumn sky. Then he is gone.

My mother kneels for days in the grass and jabs a trowel where each bulb fell. Turf splits and she drops one in and smacks the trowel down once twice three times and shuts each grass lid.

Daffodils grow and flower and lean and break in the winds that blow across our farm in the Cotswold hills. In springtime I snap off stalks and my father arrives home and shouts . . . Pick the broken buggers first old girl . . . must experiment using your brain one of these fine days . . . bloody east wind.

Fifty years later I am by Juno beach on the French Normandy coast where his Inns of Court invasion troops landed in the Second World War. Dune grass blows east and my father's wartime padre, code name Sunray, strides past in white cassock flapping in the breeze and a Hans Holbein black hat. Soldiers hold up embroidered flags on polished wooden poles tipped by fluted steel knives. The Union Jack and the French flag lie over a carved memorial stone beside a country road. War

veterans wear medals and hold flags embroidered *com-batants*. Four hundred of us stand with French families in the sun and the Inns of Court regimental band plays tunes from *Cavalleria Rusticana*.

An Inns of Court officer steps up to the dais and speaks. 'For the sake of freedom – a suicidal mission – our men never gave up – covered a wider area than any other military unit – with this act of dedication we bridge the gap between this world and the next.'

Down go the flowers. Wreath after wreath. Poppies, marigolds, daisies, phlox, poppies, daisies.

A soldier at attention by the memorial stone falls forward on his face on the grass. Two others drag his body behind the loudspeaker van. From the ranks another steps forward to take his place. The regimental band play my father's favourite hymn: 'Praise My Soul the King of Heaven' . . . and the padre reads, 'We meet in the presence of Almighty God to commemorate this day.'

Nearly all of us weep. I remember my father, with his white hair round his bald head and wearing green corduroys and a navy-blue jersey, coming past the corner of top barn, arms held open wide saying . . . Fancy our meeting . . . when times are so fleeting . . . to what do I owe the great honour of your presence on this perfect summer morning . . . what say a small celebration is in order . . . a cup of Mr Bournville's famous chocolate lightly stirred into fresh milk . . . agree . . . and I can hear my mother's voice call . . . Any shopping wanted from Cheltenham . . . I'm taking a broken bridle down . . . I'll be home by lunchtime.

The dedication of the Normandy landing regimental memorial stone is over. Soldiers march to a farm court-yard in the village of Graye-sur-Mer. Champagne and chocolate biscuits are handed out. Chocolate melts in my fingers and a French lady says to me, 'I remember the war very well, madame, we were very hungry, *oui ça c'est certain, mais* . . .' She shrugs and smiles. We look into each other's eyes and down at the melting chocolate she offers me and we laugh and she says, '*Il faut rire*, madame, we must laugh *savez-vous.*'

I say, '*Oui, merci*, it is true.'

The mayor of Graye-sur-Mer says to me, 'When I was a child I must go with no shoes. Certain things are not remembered. My family are going in the fields at night for food. It is food for cows. I do not know the names.'

I say, 'Turnips, swedes, mangolds.'

He says, '*C'est ça*. If they see us the enemy shoot.'

I say, 'Is there nothing left in the shops for you to buy?'

And he says, '*Pour les collaborateurs* ... *bien sûr*, madame, there is everything.'

A Frenchman in a black beret reaches up and embraces me and says, 'Madame, I live at Jerusalem Crossroads, a hamlet. The British soldiers come. We give them wine and flowers and tell them "Thank you." We hear aeroplanes. A soldier calls, 'It is Yanks, OK, OK, yellow – yellow.' The soldier quickly spreads yellow silk squares on the two vehicles. A yellow smoke goes up into the sky. The driver says, 'It is for the Yanks to see we are *les amis*.' The American planes fly over firing. I run away with another boy. When I return, all Jerusalem Cross-roads and all the soldiers are dead. I think I am lucky to be here with you today. It is a great honour and I say thank you, for your father. You are proud of him? I think so.'

British officer veterans drink French champagne and laugh and tell me, 'We shouldn't laugh, we oughtn't to.'

I say, 'Why not?'

They say, 'We're remembering hunting a Hun along Juno beach. Bloody hell he ran. We got him with the flail tank chains.'

I ask, 'What are flail tank chains for?'

One says, 'For mine-sweeping. Tank bars on the front swing the chains and find mines hidden under sand.'

Outside the farm courtyard I stand in wildflowers and lean on a sunny stone wall and look at a field of pale-cream Charolet cattle and hum 'Jesu Joy of Man's Desiring', and hear my father's high tenor voice descant. I see him walk across our farmyard past a downstairs window and look in. I am piling up pennies and half-pennies on his desk and *Gigi* is playing on the radiogram.

He shouts at the window . . . Turn that bloody man off . . . turn that man off . . . do you hear me . . . at once. Maurice Chevalier is singing . . . *Thank 'eaven for leetle girls . . . for leetle girls grow bigger every day . . . thank 'eaven for leet-le girls* . . . I open the window and he stammers . . . I w-will n-not . . . r-repeat n-not . . . h-have d-damned *c-collaborateurs* in m-my h-home.

I turn off the radiogram and he calls from the hall . . . That's m-more like it . . . the so-and-so should be locked up by rights . . . one first-class slippery customer . . . or after the invasion we'd have caught him fair and square. Hey-ho . . . you keep an eagle eye out for cowardly types when your turn comes old girl . . . that's my advice.

He closes the window and says . . . I hear the bastard's filthy rich these days . . . three cheers for the ignorant hoi polloi . . . now who's next on parade? What say we bring in the beloved horses and give them their tea . . . jump to it . . . enough fraternising with the enemy for you today. Did I tell you in confidence I risked the Lion of Judah over Dewpond sliprails . . . went at them like an Eleventh Hussar trooper . . . took off from his hocks . . . only had him in a rubber snaffle . . . mouth soft as a baby's bottom.

His brilliant blue eyes look my way and his finger taps his lips . . . Mum's the word . . . shh-hh . . . if I am called upon to make a confession I shall simply say to your mother . . . not a hope in hell of stopping a young horse who's made up his mind to jump a fence . . . you'll know that as well as I do. He and I walk up the yard and he sings . . . Chirri-birri-bin . . . chirri-birri-bin . . . I love you so-o . . .

At Five Acre gate he calls the horses . . . Come on . . . come on, girls and boys . . . teatime . . . teatime . . .

I climb the elmwood bars and say . . . What is a *collaborateur* . . .

He says . . . Not now . . . not now . . . keep your mind on one thing at a time . . . look out . . . here they come . . . a fine sight if ever I saw one . . . open the damned gate . . . get a move on . . . don't stand there coffee-housing like the bloody French . . . off the bars . . . I am in no mood to pay for new hinges . . . that's more like it . . . have a leg up onto Glory Boy . . . then lead on. The rest will follow . . . if we're lucky.

I ride bareback up Rickyard Lane astride my father's

tall chestnut and look over the Cotswold grey-stone wall
built on Calfpen bank to our hills and woods. He pulls
fistfuls of linseed barrel nuts out of his green corduroy
trouser pockets. Loose horses follow and push and shove
to nuzzle his pockets. We pass the twin stone barns tall as
churches and turn down into the farmyard.

My mother's Irish money buys our Elizabethan farm
in 1941, the second summer of World War Two. My
father's Inns of Court regiment is fighting a mock battle
on the Cotswold hills and from a high point he looks
down and sees what he thinks is a small village or a
hamlet in a hollow. He tells his armoured car driver . . .
Head downhill . . . we'll make a quick recce . . . His car
roars down Homefield and he finds the deserted farm.

A doll's house face under triple gables looks at a
farmyard circle of stone barns and stables spreading to

cattle sheds and lanes. A front door path is between two green squares of lawn edged by sprawling pink roses on a drystone wall. The garden swerves away past a cherry tree and south around two apple trees to the wicket gate at the damson tree by the Rushy Brook stream. The house faces north because Elizabethans believe flies spread the plague and sun shining on windows attracts flies. They are wrong. *Xenopsylla cheopsis*, the rat flea carries the plague and fleas are brought to England by black rat hosts from China.

He telephones my mother at her Corps headquarters at Camberley south-west of London and says . . . God willing I've found the Bears a home.

My mother has joined the First Aid Nursing Yeomanry

– FANYs – created in 1907 to train English girls to gallop on horseback onto battlefields and give first aid to wounded soldiers and carry the injured to field hospitals in horse-drawn ambulances. In the 1930s FANYs become a mechanised Women's Transport Service. Upper class girls drive and service transport lorries and motorbikes and chauffeur army personnel and chant:

> I wish my mother could see me now,
> With a grease gun under my car,
> Filling the differential
> Ere I start for the sea afar,
> A-top a sheet of frozen iron, in cold that would make you cry.
> I used to be in Society once,
> Danced and hunted and flirted once,
> Had white hands and complexions once,
> Now I am a FANY.

She says to me when she is an old lady . . . I was never lost or behind schedule driving my brigadier-general . . . even in the blackout on the very long journeys with no car lights, when we went from the north of England all the way down south to Devon.

My father telephones her FANY HQ in summer 1941

10th January, 1940.

F.A.N.Y. Miss. M. Lennox-Conyngham has been driving my car for a considerable period.

She is the only woman driver whom I have ever sat behind who gives me at all times absolute confidence.

George Clark.

Major-General,
Commanding, 1st Cavalry Division.

Barnby Moor,
Nr. Retford,
Notts.

and tells her . . . Steal a tank of petrol and concoct some excuse to drive down here p.d.q. This is a land of milk and honey. I give you my word. Take the London–Oxford A40 road past Burford and Northleach. On the ridge look left-handed across open country. A single clump of trees on the far horizon is the farm boundary. Stay on the A40. Look for a red iron gate in a line of beeches. If you fetch up at Seven Springs crossroads you've gone too far. The drive is half a mile of bloody awful potholes. If I'm right – and I'm damned sure I am – this is a home for us for ever. Those old boys knew how to build to last. No flies on the Elizabethans . . . and no flies on us. We'll be sheltered on all sides. The Almighty had his eye carefully on our future when the War Office boffins planned today's regimental exercise.

In their khaki uniforms in his armoured car they dash across the farm. My mother says . . . It all looks so terribly neglected . . . could there be something wrong with the land . . . I wish I knew more about these things . . . the Valley is nicely sheltered for horses . . . and the house does have lovely proportions.

White stones scatter the hilly land. Fences are broken walls or cut and laid hedges grown wild into tall bullfinch thorns. Gaps in walls are wide enough to drive a tank through. Gates and stable doors hang off hinges. Water is pumped by a windmill reservoir two miles away at Needlehole at the far end of the farm. Purple thistles and yellow poisonous charlock flower on grassland. Nettles spread inside barn doorways. Wild cats stare from stable drains. Rats run along house walls. In the drawing room a soldiers' campfire has burnt a hole in the ceiling.

My father says . . . We will rise above any minor problems . . . we're not about to start playing windy buggers. Not now we've found this heavenly place . . . quite right we're not . . . no siree. We'll invite your bank manager to a slap-up lunch at the Cavalry Club. A bank manager lunching with a bloody colonel in Piccadilly . . . he will think he is going up in the world. We'll never look back . . . you mark my words.

In September 1940 the Blitz begins and a year later my mother's Irish Georgian furniture arrives at the farm in a horsebox with her motorbike-sidecar. My father has gone north to Yorkshire to train his Inns of Court lawyer soldiers – the Devil's Own – to fight like hell when their time comes.

Her lights are paraffin oil lamps and she cooks on a knee-high coal range with a hot iron square over one oven. Her heating is paraffin stoves until she hammers a nail into a wall to hang a picture in the drawing room. My father comes home and says . . . Who'd have thought a nail going through a wall like butter would produce a magnificent Elizabethan open fireplace . . . and he sings . . . Praise my soul the King of heaven . . .

She sells her blue Rover and her motorbike and buys a Ford van painted British racing green and has her initials stencilled in gold on both doors and her Pytchley Hunt Point-to-Point Ladies Race silver fox leaping through a horseshoe is screwed on the bonnet.

My father is frustrated soldiering in England between 1940 and 1944. His Eleventh Hussar cavalry brother officers are fighting on the North African front. He is a colonel training lawyers to be soldiers. He writes home from Yorkshire barracks:

> *I can't tell you how much I miss you and our lovely home and wish I was there to help . . . and then I can't help wishing I was out there in the hunt for the Boche . . . so*

*I don't know what I want. I worry all the time you have
too much to do and work too hard. Find some woman to
help in the kitchen . . . or else it's no fun when I come
home on leave.*

*Never thought you would get the rye and the beans
planted. A week with fair weather and the land warm
with no frost and our seeds and wheat will all germinate
and we shall be established for the winter. The new saw
bench means you will be warm. Get lots of wood cut up.
Did I remind you no one must touch the machine until
covered under the Workman's Compensation Act in our
insurance policy. If someone cuts their hand off it is liable
to be expensive!*

*I miss you and everything so very much and long to
be home doing something useful. Have been on a damned
badly run armoured battle. Sent up by the General on
to the enemy's position to view the attack and give an
opinion. Such a bad show that I am at a loss what to
say or do. Came back before the end in disgust cold
and disheartened. All my love from your own lonely
Big Bear.*

She props a prayer written in Gothic script and illumi-
nated gold and blue capitals on the kitchen dresser – May
He support us all the Day long . . . Until the Shadows
lengthen and Evening comes – and reads his next letter:

. . . As it was my birthday I was allowed by the Priest to choose hymns for our Regimental Armistice Day Service. We sang 'New Every Morning Is the Love', 'Lead Us Heavenly Father Lead Us', 'Now Thank We All Our God'. I had the 'Nunc Dimittis' put in . . . the best of all those things and never heard unless one goes in the evening. I wished my Bear was with me at this time.

She learns to farm. Two thousand acres. A mile of valley. Horses, cattle, sheep, pigs, poultry. Snow in winter above the lintels of the downstairs windows. Her fingers swell. Chilblains. Long white kid gloves are wrapped round a leaky pipe in her bedroom knotted at the fingers. She has a lot to learn that no one has taught her. Accidents happen.

2

WARTIME

After two days leave at Christmas my father writes

> . . . *thank you for my very lovely and never to be forgotten*
> *first holiday in our new home and for all the happiness*
> *you have brought me. A terrible anticlimax coming back.*
> *I miss you and home as much as I used to as a small boy*
> *sent away to school. Our home is our own most perfect*
> *special Bears' castle for ever and always.*

His regiment moves further north to a barracks in Northumberland.

> . . . *your farmyard is a ballroom compared to my*
> *car parks up here. I am having cement roads built by*

*charming German Jew refugees. A Sergeant in charge is
Czech and was in an Austrian concentration camp with
20,000 others. A number were ordered to be hanged or shot
by Hess for no reason at all. He has written three times
to the Home Secretary to ask to be allowed to look after
Hess for one night!!!*

*No more news now darling Bear except to send you
all my love and to say how I long to be with you. How
splendid about the big new Esse kitchen range stove.
The perfection of our lovely home.*

In the Pittville Nursing
Home in Cheltenham, in snow,
in February 1942, she endures
a difficult birth and I am
born . . . their Little Bear. My
mother writes in her diary . . . I
did not know it would hurt so
much.

In springtime my father
sends

*. . . coupons for the calf with the usual unanswerable
form. Here I am very lonely and far from my Bears and
home. What a lovely Easter it was. Our first with our
Little Bear and our new home. Both equally lovely. It is*

heaven and we are so lucky to be so happy. I'm sure few
other people are as happy as we are. It all seems to be too
good to be true. I have bought you a lovely birthday
present Ralli-cart with yellow wheels and good tyres that
will look brand new with a coat of varnish. I hope you
will like it. When we find a nice pony and borrow a
harness it will be a topper and very smart.

A pony is tied to an apple
tree on a rope to graze
the lawn in circles and I
am placed in a wicker basket on the pony's back.
I have an eighty-year-old
nanny – Annie Nannie –
my mother's Irish cousins'
nanny forty years before. I must have looked up at
branches and apple blossom and warplanes.

Joe Rummings and Mr Griff and Mr Munday are farm
labourers too old for call-up. Landgirls are seconded
from their work at the Wills Tobacco cigarette factory in
Birmingham. A lorry load of Italian prisoners of war is
driven in for daily threshing and hoeing and fencing and
stone collecting.

Mrs Griffin walks two miles from Kilkenny three times
a week and cleans. She squeezes water out of used tea

leaves and scatters handfuls on carpets and kneels and bristle-brushes up dirt stuck to the leaves into a red dented tin dustpan. She dusts and wax-polishes Georgian furniture and scours iron saucepans and changes linen sheets and talks and talks all the time to my mother and Mrs Fish and to herself. Mrs Fish walks two miles over the fields from Needlehole to wash and iron bedsheets and clothes two days a week.

He writes

. . . so pleased to hear you are fixed up with Italian prisoners. Worrying about it on the train I didn't know how you'd manage. Have been thinking about you all day looking after our Little Bear and keeping the threshing going. Only wish I could be there to help instead of leaving it all on your shoulders. I know we are going to make a success. One always does if one's heart is really in it and

both our hearts are. All my love my darlingest. Soon a
lovely holiday together.

The prisoners of war are forbidden to speak. Lined up in the yard in dark-blue jackets and trousers, they call out to me . . . *Che bella bambina . . . cara . . . io te adoro . . . veni . . . veni qui.* A man in dark-blue uniform has a gun in a holster and shouts . . . No talky . . . allez . . . skeddadle . . . go-go . . . follow lady on horsy. My mother rides into Homefield leading the line. Each prisoner carries a long-handled hoe over his shoulder. They walk to fields of kale and mangolds and turnips and swedes to hoe out weeds along the rows. In winter the Italians rub their hands and call out . . . *È fredo in Inghilterra . . . molto molto fredo . . . è terribile . . .* and my mother smiles and says . . . Yes . . . cold . . . molto coldo.

Landgirls live in the house on the top floor. They sit in the kitchen and smoke cigarettes and cry and turn the battery wireless onto the Light Programme when my mother is not there. A landgirl called Jannie is my nanny after old Annie Nannie goes back to Ireland. My

mother barters cigarettes for herself and the girls on the black market in Cheltenham. She drives Merrylegs the dock-tailed Welsh cob seven miles down and seven back uphill every fortnight in the Ralli-cart, and trades home-made butter and fresh eggs and dead rabbits. Until the day she says to the landgirls . . . Getting us all cigarettes takes up too much time . . . I am stopping smoking . . . I shan't be buying cigarettes in Cheltenham any more for anyone.

A landgirl says . . . We'll have to get ours off the Yanks then, won't we . . . American airmen are billeted at Guiting Grange. Our landgirls walk down the lane to the pub at Kilkenny in the evenings in gumboots and flowered cotton dresses and mackintoshes. They carry high-heeled shoes and get picked up in US jeeps.

Sometimes a girl comes home in the morning late for milking. One girl cries to my mother . . . I can't have a Yankee baby . . . I told him . . . I swear I did . . . and my mother says . . . we'll have to get you back home to Birmingham somehow. She writes in her diary . . . New landgirl up the spout.

My mother is pregnant again and has an abortion in the Pittville Nursing Home in Cheltenham. She does not tell my father. After a first difficult birth she is advised she must not risk having another child.

January and February and March are terribly cold months. One March an east wind blows and the weather-vane fox above the granary gallops east for a week. My mother walks out of the house carrying her shotgun and loads two cartridges and aims at the fox. She fires both barrels and says . . . That should change things . . . We've

had enough of this cold east wind. Grey tumbler pigeons fly off the barns and circle high in the sky and the copper fox pirouettes all morning. Joe and Mr Griff and the land-girls stop in the yard and watch the twirling fox. One by one tumblers fall wings closed to a barn and glide to a window ledge. By afternoon the fox slows down facing north.

Her diary says . . . Why can't I be happy . . . I have everything I want . . . dear God . . .

He writes

> . . . *Eric Bates is having a bad turn. He has had a skin disease for months and that plus the fact that his wife is having a baby seems to have got him down. He sits by the hour with an ashen white face looking straight in front of him refusing to do anything. I try to knock some sense into him but it's pretty tricky. His wife is in Scotland and due to foal next week.*
>
> *Last night we played billiards after dinner and everyone got foxed. I broke several very old gramophone records over Basil's head and he walked round the billiard table saying 'I've never had that done to me before in my whole life' as if it happens to everyone every day. We all laughed a great deal and it does a lot of good. I get very depressed and feel almost like Eric at times.*
>
> *No more now my very special Bear. Not so very long to*

wait now till we see each other again after this lifetime
apart. Soon now I shall be with you and we will be happy
Bears together with all the spring flowers and sunshine
and trees coming out and so much to look at and see with
you. Keep your tail up. All my love my darlingest. Your
one and only Big Bear.

In the kitchen my mother hears aeroplanes and says
. . . Listen . . . listen . . . are they ours . . . out we run . . .
quick . . . look . . . look up . . . and black wide-winged
aeroplanes fly over in lines. At milking time one afternoon a single big grey plane roars low across the barns
and clears Fishpond Wood and then the sky gets smoky
over Top Field. My mother calls to Jannie my landgirl
nanny and me . . . Stay put in the milking shed . . . and
she and Joe Rummings and Griff pick up pitchforks and
run up Homefield.

They walk back down and my mother milks and
says . . . One of theirs crashed . . . you can't see properly
inside . . . what's left is on fire . . . if they were alive it
was not for long . . . I'll change Top Field name to
Airplane . . . in memory.

When a white smoke cross is in the sky after two
planes pass she says . . . I hope the cross means those
two are protected.

In daytime small planes rattle through the sky and

at night slow heavy engines drone over. I sleep in my mother's bedroom and in the dark she says . . . Poor pilots have a long way to go . . . I suppose they get lost sometimes . . . I hope this lot aren't for Birmingham.

At breakfast a landgirl comes in the kitchen and unpicks sticky muddy bootlaces listening to the news on the wireless and cries and says to my mother . . . It isn't fair . . . it isn't sodding fair . . . it's all on them . . . I'm going back home . . . I won't sodding stay here . . . Birmingham is my sisters . . . you don't know a sodding thing . . . you don't . . . I don't darn well care . . . sodding cows.

My mother says . . . I will ride down to Andoversford and send a reply-paid telegram to find out how they are . . . the west did have bad luck last night . . . I am sorry to say. In the milking shed she says to Joe Rummings . . . Very likely we'll be a girl less by afternoon . . .

And Joe says . . . She'll go back where she's from . . .

And my mother says . . . It's hard on girls sent here from a big town . . . no news so far if the tobacco factory's gone.

A small plane flies nearer and she picks me up and runs to the yard. A cloud of silver tinsel falls from the sky onto my mother's green topknot scarf. Silver hangs on my arms and on her pink linen blouse and her blue dungarees and sticks to my blonde curls. Tangled silver lands on stables and house gables and on barn roof moss. White pigs and brown hens and the one black hen and the grey Chinese geese are all silvery. Her black-and-white spaniel's floppy ears sparkle. Three horses in Homefield gallop away under falling silver tinsel. Brown apple tree branches and blue delphinium flowers and red and pink and yellow roses and the green lawn and white yard stones are sparkling.

I pick up silver. The plane flies off. Griff freewheels down the yard and silver hangs from his bicycle handles and on his flat brown cap and my mother says . . . What do you suppose it is all for Griff . . . it must be all right . . . or why would they let it out over us . . . as long as it has nothing to do with mercury . . . what on earth are they

dropping it on us for . . . so far I can't see anything that's fallen down dead . . . will you help Joe and the girls . . . I'm going in to turn the wireless on . . . you never know . . . we may get information.

In the kitchen she lifts me onto the dresser between the varnished wood wireless and glass butter churn. She turns the brown Bakelite wireless knob clockwise and behind the peacock tail material fan cut into wood a man's voice fades in crackles . . . An announcement follows . . . reception . . . repeat . . . will . . . repeat . . . expect . . . and the voice disappears. My mother leans on the dresser and puts her cheek close to the wireless and twiddles the knob and I twist silver in my fingers. She says . . . Nothing . . . Düsseldorf . . . Brussels . . . Paris . . . London . . . nothing from anywhere . . . I don't want to waste batteries . . . you can help me make butter while we listen . . . and Jannie can come indoors and stay with you while I ride round and make sure everywhere is safe.

She hugs the glass butter churn on the high red dresser top in one arm and untwists the tin screw lid and pours in cream from a wide white tin bowl and dips in wood paddles on a rod fixed into the lid . . . Thank heavens the cream is nicely cold . . . or we'd be here all day . . . it goes quicker since the Baroness calved . . . her Jersey cream is thicker than Ayrshire . . . I'll hold the jar tight and you can turn . . . stand up on the chair . . . keep your elbow level with the handle . . . or you won't get going fast enough.

The wood handle turns a cogwheel and the cogwheel ratchet teeth bite a small flat wheel that bites a third upright wheel that bites and turns the fourth wheel fixed round the paddle rod. I wind and cream swirls against glass and my mother says . . . That is going a good gallop . . . let's pray it separates.

I watch the glass for butter flecks and my shoulder aches and she says . . . I'll take a turn . . . you watch and see if I have good luck . . . that's nice . . . music. The wireless plays and she holds the churn steady with one hand and turns with the other. The music stops and a woman's voice says . . . We interrupt *Workers' Playtime* this morning with an announcement for listeners in the West Midlands.

She says . . . That's us . . . sshh . . . keep quiet and listen . . .

This is an announcement . . . there will be interference throughout today . . . allied radar operations are expected to continue . . . I repeat . . . expect interference . . . for the time being we return you to *Workers' Playtime* with the BBC Light Orchestra.

My mother says . . . That must be our silver . . . I wish they told us whether anything to do with it is dangerous

... can you see butter beginning ... it's time this cream hurried up.

I say ... Yellow bits are coming.

She says ... And they're sticking together ... in summertime cream can get too warm ... three cheers.

I say ... I see a lump ... can I churn ... and you watch?

She says ... No ... I'll keep going ... it won't be long now ...

She lifts out the butter on wood paddles and drops the lump into a white cooking bowl and rinses it under the cold tap and paddle-squeezes the lump so the water clouds. On a wet board on the kitchen table she breaks the lump into six and slaps and rolls. I lift grooved pats with two silver spoons onto white greaseproof paper laid on a blue willow pattern plate and my mother carries the plate into the larder and says ... That's done ... one each for Griff and Joe and Mrs Fish and for us and two for sale now I'm not getting cigarettes ... the coal shed cats can drink up leftover buttermilk.

In the afternoon rain begins. The cows tramp across the yard to milking and back again and my mother says ... You can keep all the silver you've already collected in your room ... do not touch any more.

My father writes

... I had such a lovely holiday with my Bear and seem to hate coming back here more every time. And now it is so horrid here into the bargain with the whole thing getting worse and worse and more and more officers and men going away. I have just got a further demand in for another ten officers making a total of twenty-seven now gone. I really don't know how I am going to carry on and keep the spirit of the Regiment up.

All my love, my darlingest. Take care of your special self and keep the home fires burning. Shall be home again soon. God bless you my Bear and our little Bear.

Someone sends my mother an anonymous note: ... Your husband behaves as if he has forgotten he has a wife. She reaches him by telephone and says ... If you prefer someone else then I do not want to be married ... that's all I shall ever say ... it is your choice and always will be.

He writes

. . . how could you say such horrible things on the
telephone . . . I have never been unfaithful to you. Don't do
that again. Ever.

He signs the letter . . . *Bertie.*

I sleep in her bedroom and in the dark I hear her
say . . . Alec . . . Alec . . . is that you?

A man's voice calls . . . May . . . May . . . are you
awake? She lights her candle and he walks in the bedroom and sits on her pink eiderdown. Gold braid rings
shine on his sleeves. He opens a leather suitcase and
hands her a cellophane packet. She pulls out stockings
and waves transparent legs and says . . . Nylons . . . Alec
thank you . . . have you really been in New York . . .

And he says . . . That Mecca for synthetic goods
designed to keep the female of the species in good heart.

He opens a square tin box full of pale-brown square
and oval shapes. In some centres is red jam. My mother
points thick chilblain fingers and takes one and says to
me . . . Biscuits . . . have a bite . . . lovely . . . mm-mmm.

Uncle Alec is my father's brother. A captain in the
Royal Navy on Atlantic Convoy duty. He says . . . The
milking herd all in good heart I trust . . . particularly my
beloved Baroness . . . and the garden . . . it is very nice
indeed to be here . . . I shall indulge in a first-class kip

and join you a.m. . . . good night my dear . . . good night monkey face.

His footsteps criss-cross the floor above and my mother's eyes grow big and dark eating sugary biscuits in candlelight. She falls asleep on her white pillows. Her nightdress is turquoise silk. Mine is yellow cotton. I shift my legs in bed and things scratch and prickle. I call out . . . Quick . . . I've got wasps . . . quick . . . in the sheets . . . quick . . .

My mother sits up and says . . . It's only biscuit crumbs . . . kneel up on the pillow. She leans over and her hands sweep the sheets and I can see her hands in the Dutch oval dressing-table mirror across the room.

My father writes

I wonder if one day we could introduce Rhododendrons to grow at home. They would look so lovely. A clump or two near the big beech trees in Fishpond Wood looking down at the house. All the new kinds. Pink and crimson.

On our latest exercise Wyndham surpassed himself by capturing a Brigadier on the enemy side and holding him prisoner . . . the poor man was driving peaceably to his brigade HQ from his house! He was needless to say furious.

I hear the great 'Monty' is fairly going wild visiting all his troops. Nobody is safe! We shall have him here shortly and you will probably have me back farming for good the week after!!

No more now, but to send all my love. It is a long time since I had one of your nice letters with all the news of home and I do look forward to them.

In the kitchen she stands me on a padded horsehair seat and shakes soil off carrots on newspaper on the table and says . . . One . . . two . . . three . . . four carrots. She tugs the oven door and pulls at a black iron pot and says . . . Listen to him growl. She pours water from the black kettle into the rabbit stew and prods pieces of pale haunch with a silver fork and screws up her nose and shoves the pot back in the oven and opens a letter.

15 March 1944. I have been on what the fortune tellers call 'a long journey'. Sent for suddenly in London and then onto the Isle of Wight. Back here very tired. Have to memorise difficult orders and maps without any notes. It is all very very interesting. Difficult and rather important problems. I am inclined to feel tired in mind and brain.

My new teeth were finished last week and now I have a dazzling smile with a complete set fixed more than firmly in my mouth. I can't get accustomed to it at all after so long playing with my loose plate. So it is hell and almost requires a spanner to get it out at night.

Your threshing results are very good. The Cotswolds may not be arable country but by good cultivations you seem to knock jolly fine crops out of that light land. Don't forget Nitro-chalk. If we get the results using it that I see up here it will give you valuable early feed for the herd while other pastures come on.

Sunday, 19 March 1944. I think I have found you a better more reliable wireless set and a carthorse. Will let you know. Have roughed off my three young horses up here and they graze out in the park by day.

In June 1944 he is in a wire pen on the Isle of Wight with his soldiers and armoured cars. On 6 June the Allied invasion of France starts and he fights ashore on Juno beach with instructions to destroy bridges on the River Orne behind the enemy lines.

In summer 1945 he comes home on leave and for the rest of his life he shouts in his dreams at night. After wartime he sleeps mostly in his dressing room next door to me. I go in and see him thrash and wave his arms in

the light of my torch. He
yells ... For Christ's sake
... Sunray ... Sunray ...
come in ... come in ...
dear God ... you bloody
Yanks ... do you read ...
do you read ... and he
weeps ... Goddam you
all.

(Sung to the tune 'D'ye ken John Peel' – eighteenth-century ballad)

D'ye ken Bertie Bingley with his face so red?
D'ye ken Bertie Bingley with no hair upon his head?
D'ye ken Bertie Bingley when he's just got out of bed
And he can't find his teeth in the morning?

T'was the crack of his two-pounder brought me from my bed
And the roar of the Daimlers which he oft-times led
For the rattle of his coax would awaken the dead,
Or Jerry in his lager in the morning.

Chorus

Ay, I ken Bertie Bingley and the rest of them too,
From the majors to the troopers they're the Devil's Own crew
And they live on porridge, whisky and stew
And they're randy as a stallion in the morning.

Chorus (repeat)

So here's to Bertie Bingley and his men the Inns of Court
For they know all the Devilry and tricks that he has taught
And here's to the day when to victory they've fought
And they're up on the Rhine in the morning.

Chorus (repeat)

I keep the torch under my pillow to light the way across my carpet and up the back passage steps into his room. I put the torch down on his chest of drawers . . . Words aren't any use . . . my mother says . . . It's only hitting him hard on the chest that wakes him up . . . there's no knowing why . . . I lean forward towards him on tiptoe. He swipes with an open hand and knocks me backwards. I fall over on the bronze-and-yellow Afghan rug in my nightdress and get up and rush at him and punch his chest.

Then his arms drop on the bed and lie still in blue-striped pyjama sleeves and his eyes open and he looks at me and says . . . Hello-hello . . . what's up . . . not asleep . . . off you go back to bed . . . into the arms of Morpheus . . . we'll have a first-rate jolly in the morning.

Sometimes I hear him shout and I stay in my bed and lean over the side and wind up the gramophone and play my four 78 r.p.m. records: 'Hang Out the Washing on the Siegfried Line' with 'Run Rabbit Run'. 'You'll Take the High Road and I'll Take the Low Road' with 'Speed

Bonny Boat'. 'Sounds from the Hunting Field' – side one and side two. When I put on 'The Teddy Bears' Picnic' I sing along with a man . . . If you go down to the woods today . . . you're sure of a big surprise . . . today's the day the teddy bears have their picnic . . . picnic time for teddy bears . . .

3

_____

MRS FISH

I put my fingers in my ears and run up the yard to the woodsaw that is screaming in the cart shed. Mr Munday pushes apple branches at circular whirling teeth spinning in and out of a slit in an iron table. A running tractor engine powers a long wide-webbed belt looped on the saw arm. As each slit log opens sawdust flies and a sawn log tumbles off the table. The saw whines until Munday feeds the branches to the spinning teeth again. I run back down the yard and unblock my ears going indoors.

In the kitchen jodhpur sweat is boiling out in a black cauldron before Mrs Fish scrubs the legs. My mother says . . . Shall we make a cake or meringues . . . I've got eggs to use up and enough sugar. I twiddle the wireless knob and see Mr Munday's knuckles knock at glass in the kitchen door. My mother says . . . Open it for him . . . there must be something he wants.

Mr Munday comes in and one hand holds the other and his brown hand-knitted vest has wet patches and he says . . . The saw had my fingers off.

My mother pushes a black saucepan off a hot Esse plate and closes the chrome mushroom lid. She picks up a tumbler off the drainer and turns a tap and fills the glass and pushes the rim at Munday's mouth and says . . . Drink some water . . . I can hold it for you . . . water will help . . . well done . . . that is enough . . . lift your hands up higher . . . up near your shoulder . . . keep as still as you can.

She tears a roller towel down the seam and tips two silver safety pins out of a jam jar by the wireless and says to me . . . Get cotton wool out of the dresser drawer. She wraps a sling round Munday's chest and sticks in a

pin at the back of his collarless shirt and a pin at the back of his elbow and looks in the sling and says . . . Give me the roll . . . and stuffs in all the cotton wool. She rinses blood off her hand under the tap and says . . . Come on . . . hurry . . . in the van . . . quickly . . . I'll get the saddle room cotton wool . . . you jump in . . . Mr Munday in the front.

I run ahead and open the van door and clamber between the front seats onto the corrugated tin floor and pull a blue-and-yellow-checked horse rug flat. Mr Munday sits down sideways in the passenger seat and faces the house and I say . . . Put your feet in Mr Munday . . . I'll do your door.

I clamber out of the van and run round the bonnet past the silver fox galloping in a horseshoe and slam his door and run back round and climb in again over the driver's seat and my mother races down the yard in her blue dungarees and blue canvas lace-ups with hard jelly soles and says . . . Good girl.

She leans over the gearstick and unrolls the white cotton wool pad in royal-blue paper and stuffs a handful inside the blue-and-white-striped towel sling. Her hands get wet and she wipes cotton wool up her fingers and drops the red-and-white sticky lump by her feet. She starts the van. She backs past pigsties and swerves by the barn. The van roars up through the gateway past granary

steps and the tractor shed's dark-green corrugated door
in bottom gear and stops at the cart shed by the tractor.

The saw whines and whirls and my mother leans over
the spinning belt to the tractor and the blade slows
down. She looks at the sawdust and kneels on one knee
and reaches under the table and picks up – once and
twice – and runs to the van and says . . . Don't look . . .
look away . . . both of you . . . and I see a fingernail black
round the rim and cuticle and cut skin end and a second
finger.

She puts Mr Munday's cut-off fingers in cotton wool
and wraps them in dirty green velvet she keeps for clean-
ing the windscreen and pushes the bundle onto the glove
ledge in front of her knees beside a torch and a spanner
and says . . . All right in the back . . . well done . . . sit on
the rug . . . you made a good start on the wood, Munday
. . . it is bad luck . . . they will take you in right away at
the hospital . . . I will make sure you are seen to . . . then I
can drive home and find Mrs Munday and bring her
down . . . does she do up at Foxcote today . . . am I right?
. . . until Jimmy comes home from school.

Mr Munday doesn't speak. The van hits potholes by
Sheep Dip hump and uphill by Five Acre and Triangle
Field. My mother steers zigzags to miss the bumps and at
the red gate on the main road she corners and changes
gear up to top on the level past Wistley Common. At

Chatcombe Hill brow she goes down into second and accelerates through the double bend along the rim of the steep drop to Chatcombe Wood edge and at Seven Springs she says . . . Look left Mr Munday . . . if you are well enough . . . anything coming on the Cirencester road . . . and he stares ahead.

She brakes and looks left to Cirencester and straight across towards Gloucester and right to Cheltenham. She takes her chance and accelerates right and free-wheels down Leckhampton Hill and says . . . Now we are moving . . . it is good luck the road is clear for us . . . the dry wood left from last winter is enough for you Munday . . . and for us . . . plus two loads for Joe . . . and for Mrs Fish . . . we can use any old there is and add the new when you are well enough to carry on . . . there is plenty to creosote for now . . . that will be easier for you . . . larch posts for Grindstone fencing . . . and stable doors . . . the creosoting will keep you going . . . I will make sure there is work for you . . . Joe can take on things that need shifting . . . how are you holding up . . . not far now.

In Charlton Kings suburbs she says . . . Shall I risk it . . . thirty miles an hour will not get us there in a hurry . . . I am going to hope for the best. She cuts the red lights at the Prestbury Gymkhana field crossroads and says . . . Needs must . . . and she and I chant . . . When the devil drives . . . and the van corners right hard and right again

onto gravel and stops and she looks back at me and says
... You stay there ... I won't be long ... I promise ... if
I have to be I will come to get you ... out you get
Munday ... we will have those fingers stitched on again
in no time ... if that is at all possible.

She walks up the hospital steps and opens the door
for Mr Munday and holds the velvet bundle in her other
hand.

Mr Munday's bloody vest comes home in brown
paper and my mother hands it to Mrs Fish and says ...
Mr Munday had a bad time ... two fingers lost on the
circular saw ... will you soak his vest ... if it dries he will
have it when he comes back from hospital ... which
hopefully will be before tonight.

She says to me ... You stay here with Mrs Fish ... I
don't know what time I will be back ... have a hunt for
eggs in the top barns ... I see one hen going in and out
... she may be thinking of sitting ... if you count six or
more in a nest we will move her into a coop ... thank
you Mrs Fish ... the wireless says afternoon weather is
uncertain ... good luck with the drying.

Mrs Fish drops Mr Munday's vest in a white enamel
bucket of cold water and colours thicken from pale pink
swirls to crimson. She turns back to the white china sink
and her Woodbine ash falls and powders my mother's
pink brassieres and silk peach camiknickers and linen

blouses and blue dungarees piled on the flagstone floor. Her orange ringlets bounce under a bright-green crocheted beret she keeps on indoors and she leans forward in hot water steam. Her splashed crossover cotton apron has flower faces and the black plimsoles she keeps in the coal shed and changes into from white rubber boots have no laces.

I go in the larder and scoop up food in my fingers. Pastry crust on rabbit pie and rice pudding from under brown skin and pale-pink rhubarb fool. I watch Mrs Fish through larder door hinges. She dangles jodhpurs on a thick wooden spoon. Dirty water trickles in the sink and she dumps the sopping wet lump on the drainer and spreads the legs and scrubs at buckskin thighs with yellow Sunlight soap.

I tip up a glass bottle of Kia-Ora orange squash and the bottle mouth knocks my front teeth and I lick hurt nerves. Three chrome thermoses for harvest teas stand in a row and under the slate shelf cider and ginger beer and Guinness brown glass bottles fill a cardboard box and a note says . . . Brown bottles – keep out of light.

I stand beside Mrs Fish at the sink and run cold water in a glass of orange squash. She hisses . . . Get me a gin then . . . go on . . . you heard. She grins and the Woodbine sticks to a lip and her teeth close on the little cigarette.

I can hear my father saying when he was home on leave . . . Here's to mother's ruin . . . and see him lift a cut-glass tumbler of gin and fizzy tonic . . . Shall we celebrate our beloved home by getting nicely foxed . . . what say you . . . how's that for the best idea the Colonel has had all day . . . and he sips from the glass and says . . . That washerwoman has been at the gin again . . . she damned well has . . . taste this . . . it's simply awful . . . watered down to cat's piss . . . she will simply have to go . . . I will not tolerate petty thieving in my house . . . I most certainly will not.

Mrs Fish puts her face close to mine . . . If I don't get my gin I'll tie these sodding jodhpurs round your neck . . . I am telling you.

Her wet red fingers open and the soap bar slips underwater. She pulls a blue-and-white stained tea towel off the Esse chrome rail and twists the linen in her hands and shoves the tea towel back and walks down the long white dining room her black plimsoles squeaking.

The dining room has a rosewood sideboard spinette. The keyboard has been sawed out and there it stands ruined and pretty at the end of the dining room and along the polished top stands Dutch and Irish and English silver. A rosebowl engraved with my mother's maiden name – 'May Lenox-Conyngham – 1936 Pytchley Hunt Ladies' Race'. Two silver cock pheasants . . . one pecking and one peering sideways. Two filigree jam pots with silver coolie hat lids and blue glass jars and a silver filigree pattern of tigers climbing flowers. Four glass decanters line up in grooved oak coasters with circular silver miniature picket fences. An Irish Waterford crystal decanter pair hold dark-crimson port and brown sherry. Two square Dutch ship's decanters hold transparent gin and tawny whisky.

Mrs Fish pours three fingers of gin and carries the tumbler and decanter to the kitchen and runs cold water in the decanter and holds the glass neck out to me and says . . . You put it back . . . go on . . . I'm telling you. Her soapy fingers slip and I catch and hug the cut-glass and tiptoe to the sideboard and say under my breath . . . Don't drop . . . don't drop . . . and think I can hear my father's voice shout . . . What the bloody hell is going on in here . . . I damned well want to know . . . speak up.

Mrs Fish drinks half a glass of gin and leans on the kitchen table and coughs. Her coughs are rough and brittle. I go out of the kitchen door and run up the yard slopping orange squash on dandelions and stones.

Outside the harness room the mounting block is a two-step concrete throne in sunshine. Behind a creosoted stable door horses' shoes scratch cement and straw shifts under a pony's feet. A crow flies over to Fishpond Wood. My father's horse kicks a pine partition plank and

splinters break. A horsefly comes at my face and swerves.
My black pony hangs his head over a half-door and sighs
and pricks his ears. I see creosote blister on stable doors
facing south. Mrs Fish carries a clothes basket out of
the kitchen door and weaves up coal shed cinder path
and drops the basket. A forked ash pole props the washing line and Mrs Fish gives the pole a slap so the fork
slides down the wire and the line sinks. She flings wet
clothes up over the wire and clips stripped bark hazel
pegs on overlaps of jodhpurs . . . knickers . . . blouses . . .
brassieres . . . nightdresses . . . vests . . . dungarees. She
stands on two sawn-off logs and throws white sheets up
and over and steps down and tugs the sheets flat along
the wire. Under the oak branches she does a dance with
the forked ash pole to hoist the line and the wet clothes
rise up and flap between the tree and coal shed roof.

I go in the stable and dandy-brush dust out of the black
pony's silky summer coat and finger yellow wavy dandy
bristles and hold up my hand in sunlight strips of dust. I
hear Mrs Fish's gumboots flap up the stable path and she
looks in over the half-door . . . You can take me back
home now . . . get him out . . .

I say . . . No thanks . . .

And she says . . . Get him out here . . . I'm telling you.

She slams back the barrel bolt and the pony's head
jerks up and I push his face in a webbing halter and

lead the pony. Mrs Fish steps up on the mounting block under swallows playing in the blue sky. She lifts one white gumboot and hops a circle on her other foot and says . . . Come on then . . . bring him close . . .

And I say . . . I've got to get on first.

I vault on off the ground and ride past the mounting block and she steps behind me across the pony's broad back. We turn out of the yard and start down Rickyard Lane. White elder flowers big as saucers lean over stone walls on either side. Mrs Fish begins to sing . . . If you were the only boy in the world, and I was the only girl . . . in a sweet, husky treble and I groan.

At Fiveacre gate the stream parts clumps of gold kingcups and goes under the lane and oak and ash and larch grow along steep slopes either side and the path gets darker. Low branches stretch across and meet. The pony walks in hardly any light. Mrs Fish finishes singing 'God Save the King' and begins . . . If you walk through a storm hold your head up high and don't be afraid of the dark . . . and we come to the wide-open Valley gate. The pony trots across baked mud ruts and starts to canter on the grass and I yell . . . I can't stop him . . . and Mrs Fish shouts close to my ear . . . Let him go then.

Her bony arms are tight round my waist and her fingers hold a butcher's grip. The galloping pony rocks. I pull up my knees and crouch and grip mane hair in both hands and hold the halter rope. Mrs Fish leans her chest on my back.

The pony gallops flat out over Valley cowslips and thistles. Rabbits run past bluebells and disappear down warrens in trees. Hoofbeats rumble and jays scream. A pigeon swerves above us as we race down the long bright-green strip. Where the woods end a chaotic plan of anthills circles Alexandra's Gorse hillside. Green tumps bulge high as the pony's knees and at a tall one the pony swerves downhill. Gravity pulls Mrs Fish sideways and she hugs me tightly. Her thighs slip. Our bodies cling and wobble and our legs stick out sideways and wave.

Mrs Fish and I fall . . . rolling over gorse twigs . . . stuck by green gorse needles . . . squashing yellow gorse flowers . . . red ants scurry . . . lucky for us ancient grass is spongy. We sit up side by side between anthills puffing hard. Downhill the pony pulls couch grass and mows small brilliant blue speedwell flowers and Mrs Fish says . . . Go on then . . . fetch him up here.

A rabbit skims a gorse bush and scuds uphill to the

wicket gate and the flowering horse-chestnut tree and the pony's head comes up and his ears prick.

I say to Mrs Fish . . . Stand on an anthill . . . and I tug the pony up close and say . . . Bend your knee . . . one two three . . . and I lift her foot and she lands astride. I jump off the bouncy anthill behind her.

The pony walks to the Valley end and I see smoke from Mrs Fish's cottage and above Windmill blackthorn spinney grey windmill blades spin on a frame of legs and bars. Mrs Fish sings hymns – 'For Those in Peril on the Sea' and 'All Things Bright and Beautiful' and 'And Did

Those Feet in Ancient Times' – up to Needlehole Cottages. In the paddock the scent of dead lilac and cow-parsley and wood and stone blow past and I slide off and Mrs Fish swings her gumboot across the pony's neck. She sits side-saddle and slips down and I pull the pony round the way we came. Mrs Fish says . . . I'll have a ride back after Betty comes in for tea.

She hauls a split elm rail across the paddock track and pokes it in a horseshoe nailed on the gatepost and says . . . I'll fetch water . . . you let him go.

Dog roses grow up broken walls and stick through

empty pigsty windows. Orange marigolds flower against a dark-green water-butt. Mrs Fish drops in a wooden bucket for water. The pony pulls at roses. Mrs Fish shouts . . . Get him off the flowers.

She throws a stone so the wall rings. The pony backs away. She lugs the bucket up the garden path and water slips inside her white rubber boot. The pony drinks and huffs. His breathing starts a whirlpool in the bucket. He sucks and gulps and his long top hairstar lip wipes inside the rim and the bucket falls over and rolls and rattles. His front legs rear up towards Halfmoon Spinney and he prances along the trees with his nostrils flared and his tail crooked high. He halts and his knees and hocks fold and he sinks on the grass and rolls and chucks his body side to side and gallops his legs upside down. He sits front legs straight and stands and shakes his skin and starts to graze.

Mrs Fish says . . . You come along indoors.

I cross my legs and stand still. She opens the blue front door and looks round and shouts . . . The privy's round the back.

I hear water pour and wood fall inside the cottage. I can't see past geranium flowers and green leaves clambering up smeared window-panes. I go along a grass strip between carrot rows and peas twined in hazel sticks to a corrugated-iron hut. I shove my finger in an opening and lift a wire hook. Inside the hut torn newspaper hangs on mouldy green string and a circle is cut in board on a box and down the hole is black water and floating brown lumps and the smell's sweet rotted muck. I hunch off dungaree straps with my thumbs and shove down white cotton knickers and sit on the damp wood ring and shut my eyes tight. I can hear piss splash and see pink garden worms and shiny grey slugs crawl on my skin.

I don't touch the paper flaps. I hoist up knicker elastic and trouser bib and one strap and lift the hook and run along the grass path strip.

Mrs Fish's lovely daughter Betty comes in the garden gate. She is taller than Mrs Fish. Her auburn hair shines in the sun. She wears a white cotton puff-sleeve blouse and daffodil-yellow full gathered skirt and white ankle socks and slip-on black elastic plimsoles. Her blue eyes look my way. She smiles my father's smile and says . . . You coming in?

I don't follow her. In the paddock the backs of my legs press the drystone wall. I pick off yellow lichen cushions and hear chair legs  scratch brick floor. The sun goes in. Swallows fly low over the two cottage chimneys. The cold breeze raises goose bumps on my skin. I lean on the pony's withers and fold my arms and put my cheek on my hands and when he steps I step.

Rain begins. I turn over the water bucket and step up and spring off onto the pony and whack his neck with the halter rope knot.

He stops grazing and I pull his head away from the cottage and whack his shoulder again and again and we jump the paddock sliprail and gallop down the stony lane. His ears lie back and he catsprings from green verge to centre strip. I sit tight. Soaking wet we gallop flat out beside a field of blue lucerne and he slides to a stop at top valley gate.

I leave the valley at Hilcot Lane by the stream. The rain gets less. Birds flicker in trees. A dog rose pricks my ankle bone. The pony's hooves slap stone. His tail whisks and slips off his backside. His head pulls down to graze

and the rope knot jerks my fingers loose. He swipes at grasses and I hear him munch the tangled stalks.

At Hilcot Ford he walks in the water and drinks and cold fills my shoes. I slither off and my dungaree legs soak darker blue. In my pockets sugar lumps are syrup. Two green dragonflies dive and cling head to head. Four white ducks quack. I pick the halter rope out of the water and pull towards the elm plank bridge and stand and jump and land lying across the pony's back and wriggle and twist and sit up.

Churchbells ring the other side of Hilcot Hill and from the top I see cars outside the churchyard wall. I ride down and knot the pony's rope to the churchyard gate and tiptoe over dandelions and gravel. I twist the iron ring and push the door and hear words from prayers . . . Beloved . . . born again . . . for ever . . . amen . . . and singing . . . the Lord is my shepherd, I shall not want . . .

A thick red velvet curtain is behind the oak door. I breathe in dust behind. People wear black in the three front pews and flowers are laid on a purple cloth. The singing stops. A parson speaks muffled words. I can't breathe. I press my thumb hard on a nail head in the oak door. I think I hear a voice say . . . Out you come, monkey face . . . no time like the present.

At the churchyard gate the pony dozes. I hug an arm round his face and my other arm across his neck and pull

his head close to my chest. Men I don't recognise carry a coffin out on their shoulders and through the church-yard. On the church roof drainpipe a gargoyle grins. I jump on the pony and kick his sides and trot and bump bareback down the road and turn in the Abells' Hundred Acre grass field.

Skylarks sing and the pony gallops high above Foxcote village. I crouch forward and pull my knees up racing. I canter on Roughill Lane and trot past Keeper's Cottages and Valley gate and the vegetable garden and up Rickyard Lane slope. In the stable I pull off the halter and wriggle the bolt shut and sit on the mounting block and hear milk buckets clang. My mother looks up the yard from top cowshed doors and calls . . . Come and give a hand . . . Mrs Fish has gone home . . . no one seems to be about.

4

COWS

Early one May morning I hear below my bedroom window my mother's footsteps run to the house from the milking shed. The kitchen door slams. I run onto the landing and see the blue of her summer dungarees flash past stair banisters. She runs into the drawing room and swoops up her orange silk knitting bag off the sofa by tortoiseshell handles and turns and races back the way she came. I run eight steps down . . . jump four . . . run eight . . . jump four . . . on crimson stair carpet and she calls over her shoulder . . . Put boots on.

At the back door I sit down on flagstones and tug at gumboots and get up and run across the yard. The milking shed is empty and sun shines through Cowpath door. Boots squelch muck up Cowpath slope and bare

feet slip in rubber and my long yellow spotted cotton nightdress Mrs Griff sews with a half-inch white broderie anglaise hem frill winds around my knees. I see my mother leave Cowpath at Grindstone wall corner. I follow her and see a gap in Grindstone wall. All across Grindstone lie brown and white humps. Thirty Ayrshire cows laid flat out in clover and Baroness the one brindle Jersey stands and gasps by the wall.

My mother runs to the nearest cow and kneels and lays her face on the swollen belly. She kneels up straight and picks a knitting needle from the orange silk bag. On one knee in an archer's pose she raises her hands with the knitting needle up above her head. She says to me . . . Keep well back . . . She stabs the stomach. The needle point disappears in the cow's skin. The needle goes in as far as her fingers. She leans forward and pulls and stink whistles out of the hole. I step away and she stands up and goes to the cow's face and rubs and says . . . Come on Bluebell . . . get up . . . come on now . . . hup . . . hup . . . c'mon . . . c'mon . . . up you get girl . . . on your feet . . . there's a sweetheart . . . c'mon . . . c'mon. The cow raises her heavy head off the grass and lurches upright and stands. My mother runs to the next-nearest cow and I pick up the orange silk bag and follow. She kneels and stabs and pulls out her knitting needle and stands up and runs and I rub each cow's face and say . . . Come on . . . hup you get . . . hup . . . Prudence . . . Corralie . . . Snowflake . . . Jealous . . . Vera . . . and we run and kneel and stab and run and rub cows' faces and call their names . . . Marigold . . . Pansy . . . Special . . . Hesperus . . . Our footsteps make silver lines in green clover.

One by one the milking herd stand and follow one after another to the gap in the wall. They step over the fallen stones and go down Cowpath to the milking shed and into the byres. Three times my mother kneels by a cow and calls to me . . . She is not breathing . . . leave her. Marigold and Jumper and Whitey lie dead in clover.

At half past seven when Joe Rummings freewheels his bike down the yard into top cowshed my mother is

milking on a three-legged stool. Rich clover milk spurts fast and thick onto galvanised iron. I lug buckets into the dairy and bubbles slip over the rim and warm milk runs into my boot under my toes.

My mother calls out ... Good morning, Joe ... will you take over the cooler for me ... we've had trouble ...

the herd broke through into Grindstone clover ... we've lost three blown ... twenty-eight saved and standing ... I am milking enough for an army ... I will need an extra churn sterilised ... they had bet-ter stay put until we get

62

hurdles into the gap . . . or else we will be saving them all over again later.

Joe says . . . I reckon you'll take a cup of my tea this morning.

My mother says . . . Tea will be lovely, Joe . . . thank you.

He unbuckles his canvas knapsack and unscrews the white Bakelite lid off a green thermos and pours black tea and tips milk and sugar out of two screwtop jam jars and stirs with a penknife blade.

My mother says . . . Put the cup on the partition wall Joe please . . . I will keep going while the tea is cooling . . . I wonder if either landgirl is coming this morning. A girl in a mob cap and gumboots comes down the shed buttoning up a long white coat and my mother says to her . . . Start off with Vera . . . she won't be easy today . . . stay nice and quiet . . . rest your fore-

head against her . . . that way you'll hear a kick coming . . . hold onto the bucket . . . if a stool goes over nothing is lost . . . saving stool and bucket never happens.

The cow's kick is too quick and the landgirl

jumps back and over go stool and bucket and milk trickles and thins down the shed. The landgirl says . . . Bloody stupid cow . . . kill you . . . I will . . . what you playing at . . . sodding hate you cows . . . God I hate the lot . . .

And my mother says . . . Try to keep your temper . . . swearing blue murder only upsets the others . . . save unspilt milk.

The landgirl holds the wooden seat to her bum and sits. As she puts down the stool her other hand pulls the bucket between her knees and she says to the cow . . . Stay still now Vera . . . that's a girl . . . come on darling . . . come onto me now . . . give over Vera . . . be a lover . . . you're my own sweetheart . . . keep still for me won't you.

That day my mother lists the total gallons in her tall straight handwriting in the Milk Marketing Board book. The figures turn out at the end of her ten years' milking to be the highest yield she ever recorded. I say to her years later . . . Doesn't a cow have four stomachs . . . how did you know exactly where to pierce . . . and she says . . . I listened for sounds of clover fermenting.

On the mornings I get up and go out with my mother she says to me in top milking shed . . . Wait here. I hear her broom back bang cement floor and she sings . . . For all the Saints, who from their labours rest . . .

If I squeeze in a gap between the roller doors I can watch her lever up rat trap hinges with a stick of elder. She wears leather gloves and pulls at a dead rat slammed nearly in half by guillotine wire. Blood drips off rat skin on her  glove leather and she sees me over a partition and says . . . I said you are not to come in . . . rats are horrible . . . do not watch . . . go outside . . . you heard what I said . . . I mean this minute . . . or else stay in your room . . . and besides that . . . you are not to go looking in Calfpen later . . . not nice . . . do not do it. Calfpen is where Joe throws dead rats in the kingcup bog.

I sit on a black feed bin and rub a finger along stencilled white letters – R. A. BINGLEY – ELEVENTH HUSSARS – and open the lid and climb in and let down the lid on my hands. I lie in rolled oats and pick torn silver paper lining off cracks to let light in. A second landgirl arrives and the two girls slide bums onto the bin and light cigarettes and I can hear them talk.

Where've you been?

Not telling yet . . . am I.

Cows are done . . . you'll get a telling.

Don't care do I . . . she's a cow.

Dare you.

Time someone told her.

What's that inside . . .

Don't know . . . get off . . . we'll soon see.

The landgirls look down at me and say . . . What you in here for . . . little sneak you are . . . come on . . . get out . . . keep your trap shut . . . or else we'll put you in along with the old rats . . . she'd never mean it . . . blamed well do.

The girls go down the cowshed yawning and my mother comes out and says . . . Try not to be late tomorrow. I sit on the feed bin lid and say to her . . . There's a mousie inside . . . listen . . .

And she says . . . I haven't time . . . jump off . . . quick . . . and she lifts the lid and I hang my head over the pinewood rim and scoop rolled oats in a tin hat ladle and into a bucket. She scoops linseed nuts from the next bin along and carries two buckets from byre to byre. I tip one heaped measure into thirty-one split-drain curved ochre mangers licked shiny by cow tongues. I step up on manger edges and ride partition walls and slide down and she walks round and we measure out cow feed for afternoon milking.

After school before tea I lift the latch on Cowpath door and the herd tramp past. Horns push and shoulders shove and the cows' big brown eyes are starey with long-ing. Pink teats are fat and stiff and udders bump dry muck on hocks.

I hug a cow's soft dewlap neck and my fingers reach for chains nailed to byre walls. The cow's head goes down and her sopping wet nose burrows the man-ger. Her head swerves up and she chews cow feed to cud and brown spittle bubbles her lips. I lean against her neck and  shoulder and pull rusty chain ends. I link a key bar in a ring and shove my shoulder against her ribs to squeeze a path out between her and the other cow in a double byre. If my mother is not watching I tiptoe along the manger in front of a cow's face and horns and climb a byre wall. Sometimes a rough tongue swipes my face or a horn bangs my chest. We chain up thirty-one cows. Twice a day. Morning and afternoon. My mother will not let me learn to milk. She says . . . Look at my hands . . . this is what milking does. Her fingers are swollen crimson and chilblains crack open knuckle skin. I sit astride a partition wall and kick whitewash flakes on the ground and chew cowcake nuts and suck out the oil and spit husks at criss-cross lines grooved on the concrete floor. One line twitches and runs. I call . . . A rat . . . over there . . . there . . . look . . . quick.

My mother leans back on the three-legged stool to look round the cow's udder. A galvanised-iron bucket falls and clanks and a landgirl's white mob cap rises above the cow's back and milk runs to the drain and my mother says to the girl . . . There isn't a rat . . . take the bucket to the dairy and rinse it carefully . . . wash both hands and start again . . .

And I say . . . There was . . . I saw it.

The landgirl walks by and rattles the bucket handle and I look away up at a skylight's lichen smears. In the dairy I hear iron slam slate and tap water run. The landgirl comes back and milk whines into the empty bucket and bubbles onto shallow milk and slowly the sounds grow lush and deep.

When milking is done I unlink chains and cows stumble backwards out of double byres and a curved horn jolts against anthill hips and cloven hooves slip on wet concrete and muck. A cow's head goes down as she slides and staggers and her horns swing and poke an udder. My mother and the landgirl and I slap and shout . . . Get up, Vera. Come on, Rose. Move over. Give Lilah room. Hold back, Lilah. Back. Rose, now get over. You stupid cow . . . g'wan . . . g'wan.

A landgirl unhooks a thick black rubber hose and

spews cold water into each byre corner. Water wrinkles back and flows down the centre slope and cow dung and urine are swept along in an oily lake. The girl pushes a big beechwood bristle broom in grooved wet shiny cement channels and outside the door the muck lake falls off Cowpath into Calfpen Field where kingcups thrive and dead rats are thrown.

Inside the dairy slate slabs are cold all the year. My mother raises the two-gallon bucket in a trophy lift to fill the milk cooler. Her body strains and she leans back on her heels as if the wind is there to hold her. One hand grips the rim. The other tips up the bucket base. Milk pours in the funnel mouth and rolls over and little waves bump and curl behind a green glass window strip. A brass tap hangs off the tin tank below over a five-gallon churn. The churn lid lies upside down on a slate shelf broad as a brimmed hat.

Her fist thumps brim lid into churn. She stands legs apart and tips leaning the full churn towards her and hauls the handle epaulettes in arcs so the churn iron base scrapes the dairy floor and she peg-leg walks and sways out of the dairy door.

Three churns are full and Joe Rummings backs the tractor down top milking shed concrete to the dairy. I lift up the two-wheeler tow bar. Joe backs to me. We match up the tractor draw-bar holes. I drop in the one-eyed pin and push over a safety clip on a chain. He and my mother hoist the churns by the handles onto the trailer platform. Joe backs up the centre slope looking round at the tow-bar joint and the double doors out to the yard and steers the two-wheeler dead straight. Potholes shake the trailer so churns chime and the linch-pin flinches up the half-mile drive. At the red iron gate Joe steers beside a timber platform built on stilts and rolls each churn off the trailer. Twice a day a Milk Marketing Board lorry turns in on its way to Gloucester Dairies and picks up. My mother won't allow landgirls to drive the milk trailer up to the gate ever since one girl got off the tractor and jumped into a milk lorry with the driver and never came back.

I say to my mother ... Can the Baroness have a

riding lesson ... and she says ... Once round the yard ... that's all.

The little Jersey cow leaves the milkshed last behind thirty-one tall Ayrshires and I pull a pony halter over the short curved horns and stroke her brindle dished face and mealy nose and my mother says ... No wonder Uncle Alec loves her ... she is very pretty . . . such a good girl . . . see her secret black thumbprints in her ears. I jump to lie across her back and wriggle and sit and take the halter rope and pull the cow's head away from Homefield and up the yard and back down and say . . . Can we try putting on a saddle . . . her bones hurt . . . and my mother says . . . No . . . ride a pony instead.

A man in leather gaiters and a wide brown hat trots a grey cob down the yard and she says . . . Uncle Frank . . . how good to see you . . . have you any time to spare . . .

The first time he ever rode into the yard he said to her . . . Frank Fletcher . . . Andoversford Cattle Market . . . I heard you're up here on your own . . . you'll come down to the market for calves I take it . . . any way I can give a hand . . .

She said . . . That's very kind of you . . . it's calves I am uncertain about . . . when to buy and sell . . . how many weeks old.

He said . . . You'll have heard of the Herod plan.

She said . . . No . . . I don't think I have.

He said . . . Every steer calf sold by seven weeks the government pay a third over market price.

She said . . . That's very young to wean a calf, isn't it . . .

He said . . . Wartime . . . meat's wanted quick . . .

come down early to my house . . . back of the auction ring . . . I'll be glad to put a deal your way.

She says . . . Will you come indoors . . . I've stabling for the cob . . .

Andoversford Market is on Fridays. My mother takes me into Frank Fletcher's house behind the auctioneer ring and sits me on his windowsill and says . . . You stay put here in Uncle Frank's . . . there's too much going on in the cattle yards . . . you might get hurt. The room is brown and smoky. The window is small. I click pewter tankard lids and look out at the auctioneer call . . . Who will start me . . . four nice calves . . . six and seven weeks . . . now what am I bid . . . get started . . . I haven't got all day . . .

My mother lifts a brown-and-white heifer calf she's bought into the back of the van and says to me . . . In you get . . . good . . . now you hold onto her tight . . . don't let her move. The back doors shut and the engine starts and wheels bump out of Uncle Frank's gate onto the road.

I stroke the calf and say . . . Be a good girl . . . keep still . . . it's not far to go. Uphill passing Kilkenny the van back doors swing open. I hug the calf's neck and say . . . No you don't . . . you stay in here . . . don't you try to get up. The calf struggles and slips backwards and on the flat after Cold Comfort Farm the calf and I slip together

over the edge of the van and roll down into a ditch.
The calf kicks and I lock my arms tight. We lie in nettles
and water.

I hear the van drive away and then drive back and
stop and my mother says . . . What on earth happened to
you two . . . I was halfway to the red gate before I heard a
back door banging and I stopped to have a look and
you'd both gone.

I say . . . You said hold on . . . I'm all stung . . .

She says . . . Be brave . . . let's get you both back in . . .
no bad damage done . . . I'll put vinegar on your stings
. . . that'll calm them down. We lift the calf back in the
van and I climb in and she clicks the door handle twice
and says . . . You'll be safe this time.

Calf pens are at the back of the cowshed next to Big
Barn. I climb a hurdle and three calves skip in straw and

bump me with their heads. I hold out fingers and the new calf sucks and pulls and my finger skin hurts. A land-girl carries a bucket of fresh warm milk and bran gruel and pours shallow pans half full. I keep my fingers in the calf's mouth and put my hand in the milk. The calf sucks and I pull my fingers out. The two other calves stick noses in to slurp and bubble. In early summer cows in Homefield call their calves all night and day and weaned calves in calf pens call back.

5

YARD

Joe Rummings opens the kitchen door and says . . .
There's a two-wheeler tyre to go down.

My mother says . . . Thank you, Joe . . . can the tyre
wait . . . petrol coupons are low.

Joe says . . . There's two oil tins empty . . . and a pair of
paraffin . . .

And she says . . . I understand . . . load them in the van
if you will please, Joe . . . I'll drive straight down to the
garage after lunch.

She carries her gun on her arm up Homefield to Rushy
Bank and from Ratshill to Airplane she holds the loaded
twelve-bore in both hands her thumb on the safety catch
and her trigger finger ready to fire. The black-and-white
spaniel runs close behind her leather lace-up ankle boots.

I walk behind the dog and she whispers ... Keep your feet off twigs. A pigeon flies high across Ratshill Wood corner and heads for Chatcombe and my mother raises the gun. She puts the walnut stock between her shoulder and neck and squints along the barrel and swings up the gun over the hedgerow.  The dog and I stop in our tracks. The pigeon veers sharp left over the dew pond. My mother fires. The pigeon zigzags and a second barrel bangs. The bird's wings glide and flutter, and the body tumbles head first and hits spring wheat in Airplane Field.

Her thumb clips the barrel catch sideways and she picks out and drops two empty brass-ended orange cartridge cases. She reaches in her pocket and puts two full cartridges in the barrels and snaps the stock shut.

The spaniel shivers and her stub tail wags her black bottom and my mother says ... Seek him out ... good dog ... seek ... seek him then. The dog casts circles in green wheat and snuffles and halts and shuffles the pigeon in her mouth and trots back grinning. My mother says ... Drop ... drop it ... good dog ... let it go ... good dog ... and pulls string from her pocket and knots the bird's neck at the white feather ring. The grey-blue head lolls on mauve breast feathers. I loop the string in my fingers and she says to the dog ... Come to heel ... heel ... quiet ... sshh ... we will try our luck once more.

Rabbits and pigeons hang along the white-washed wall in Paraffin Shed. My mother says ... Let's hang up today's and take a hung bird down and get it over with.

In the kitchen I lay newspaper and a board on the scrubbed wood kitchen table and she cuts the head and feet and plucks feathers that stick to her hands and float over the Esse cooker. Her fingers claw out undigested grain in the pigeon's croup and pull intestines and liver and heart out backwards from the stomach. She leaves in kidneys and neatly bends legs and wings. I knot white string and smear soft yellow butter on purple skin. I fold newspaper over pigeon feet and innards and head and carry the parcel up coal shed cinder path and pull a wood square off an oil barrel and drop the parcel over the edge.

The rubbish barrels stink to high heaven. Once a week Joe rolls full barrels up a plank onto the two-wheeler and drives to Valley far-end quarry. He tips out a muck of fur and tins and glass and papers and brings back filthy empty barrels. My mother throws eggshells and bones and vegetable parings in a tin bucket to stir in pigswill every morning.

One lunchtime she pulls a roasting tin from the hot oven and lifts a pigeon on a willow pattern dish. She and I sit in the dining room and she says . . . Don't bite down hard . . . shot's hidden in this bird . . . plums and custard for pud . . .

And I say . . . Is it runny custard . . .

And she says . . . My time ran out and I had cold custard all ready set . . . three spoonfuls . . . or else you stay put at the table till teatime. So make up your mind to eat up if you want to come to Jack's.

The green van freewheels downhill past Kilkenny and into Jack's garage in Andoversford and she sings . . . All things bright and beautiful, all creatures great and small; all things wise and wonderful, the Lord God made them all. By the corrugated-iron shed she says . . . Wait here . . . I'll look for Jack. Out of the van window I see a dapple-grey showjumper in a head-collar gallop past the alley beside the garage shed and Jack running behind shouting . . . G'wan . . . g'wan . . . git-hup . . . git-hup. I get out and crouch up the alley and hide behind a black oil drum and dark-green summer nettles and I see Jack's showjumper

City Lights lying flat out on his side on the grass by a furze jump fence. Jack kneels on the horse's neck and cheek. Two garage boys pull and tug a chain clear from the horse's hind legs. Jack stands up and says . . . G'wan . . . g'wan my son.

The horse's head slants up off the grass. His eyes roll black and white and up comes his body and his forelegs splay and shove the ground. His hindquarters lurch as he hauls upright and stands four-square. His shoulder skin quivers and his ribs blow and his head goes high. Jack threads a head-collar rope under his chin and the horse jerks back.

Jack pulls the rope and the horse walks after him past the alley and up the paddock away from the furze fence. The garage boys stretch the chain level along the jump the far landing side. A boy stands at each post and holds the chain below the horse's sight. Jack pulls the horse towards the furze and slips the rope and whips the horse and throws clods and stones. The horse canters along the wall and Jack shouts . . . G'wan . . . g'wan . . . and thrashes at grass. The grey horse gallops and takes off at the fence. Jack shouts . . . Do it . . . do it . . . The horse's front legs lift. The boys raise the chain and as the horse jumps the boys let go and I hear links rattling and see the horse's knees buckle. He starts falling. His head slides along grass, scattering red dockweed seeds, he is pulled down by the tangled chain in his legs. Rapping is to make a horse learn to jump higher.

My mother calls out . . . Where are you . . . have you seen Jack or the boys . . . they've disappeared . . . what on earth are you doing crouched down there . . .

And I run to her and say . . . Jack is chain-rapping City Lights.

The boys walk towards us with their hands and wrists deep inside oily blue dungaree pockets and I say to my mother . . . Don't talk to Jack.

She says . . . Don't be silly . . . sit in the van if you don't want to come . . . and walks fast across the paddock. Her canvas shoes kick dock leaves and I follow and keep looking down. Jack leads the dappled grey horse away to a stable and my mother calls . . . Hello Jack . . . I've brought down a punctured two-wheeler . . . how goes City Lights . . . those knees look nasty . . . and his hind legs . . . you'll want to get that all healed before Cheltenham Show . . . the vet's up at the farm tomorrow to a ringworm calf . . . I can send him back via you . . . I'll ask the boys to take the tyre out . . . and fill up two paraffin and two oil . . . I'll pick up the tyre tomorrow morning before lunchtime and bring you the *Horse & Hound* they say rapping is soon to be banned . . . no entry in any class for a horse showing signs . . . I must hurry now . . . we are short of wind again . . . goodbye for today Jack and thank you . . . good luck with City Lights.

In the van I say . . . What will happen . . . and she says . . . It is such a pity . . . City Lights could've jumped a house if asked to before Jack set to work . . . you can't train a horse that way . . . you break his spirit . . . qualifying him for White City is out of the question . . . that is where the big money is . . . at international showjumping level . . . Jack paid over the odds for a horse to showjump for cash . . . I'll put my eye-teeth on City Lights being up for sale before autumn . . . things change quickly when money enters in . . . people like Jack have got to learn . . .

And I say . . . Then we'll buy City Lights . . .

And she says . . . No . . . showjumping is not our world . . . it is all designed for the hoi polloi. Look . . . the Cold Comfort sisters are out in daylight . . . they must be running short of water . . . their spring is across the main road . . . pray they don't get bowled over . . . nowadays cars travel a great deal faster . . . especially at night-time when the old girls come out more often.

Two women in black dresses and black rubber boots cross the road. The tall thin one carries a wooden yoke across her shoulders and chains hook onto white enamel buckets. The hem of her dress is above her knees at the back.

My mother brakes and says . . . You can ride over

81

to the windmill with me if you saddle up quick when we get back.

Her half-thoroughbred chestnut mare and my roan Welsh pony trot over Homefield tractor ruts into Rushy Bank. We canter beside the bog to Ratshill and gallop across stubble to the Bogden wicket gate. In Bogden

Wood the mare slides on hocks down a steep clay path and the pony treads short steps behind. At a sharp bend by the badger sett the mare's back leg slips in a badger earth and my mother pulls her up short and tightens the reins and says . . . Look where you are going . . . that was very silly . . . I do not want any broken bones . . . concentrate properly from now on. At the bottom the mare jumps a single sliprail between brambles and my mother calls over her shoulder . . . Keep him going . . . use your legs. The pony takes off close and cat jumps and I lose my stirrups and bounce off the saddle and land sitting on boggy grass. My mother canters alongside the loose pony and leans down and catches the reins and leads him back and says . . . Get

set . . . jump up . . . all's well that ends well . . . you let him take off too close for comfort . . . next time push on sooner.

She trots uphill past the windmill blackthorn spinney and dismounts and threads the mare's reins between plain wire strands to loop over a larch post and says . . . I'll tie her up . . . she is afraid of windmill noises . . . you look after yourself.

The windmill is fenced in among brambles and high above us the sail-arm creaks. The mare lays her ears flat and jerks back her head and reins snap tight. My mother strokes the white blaze and says . . . You be a good girl . . . I have to look after the windmill . . . a breeze has got up and that's good news . . . I won't be long . . . you stand quiet . . . there's nothing to be afraid of . . . my lovely girl.

A criss-cross galvanised steel tower narrows up to a platform high above the top of the spinney. My mother climbs rungs up five ladders and stands on the platform. An arm's length above her head grey tin blades are whirling. The sail-arm swipes south to east and the blade face follows. The sail-arm and the face swing back and the windmill turns slowly till the sail-arm swings across again to the east.

My mother stands feet apart. She bends and her hands grip a rusty Z-pipe handle. Her arms and shoulders pull and tug. Cogwheels click past slots. The sail-arm swipes and pulls the windmill face. Grey blades keep on circling fast after she locks the arm-wheel cogs. She stands up and hollows her back on her hands. Windmill blades whoosh close to her head and loose screws jingle-jangle. She looks up and looks down over the platform rail and waves and smiles.

Coming down the ladder she calls . . . You can help me measure . . . tie up . . . go three posts further along.

The water reservoir tank is sunk between the four windmill legs. I hand her a bent hook and she lifts and drags aside the square iron lid. We lie down on opposite sides of the tank and look into a deep black hole and she says . . . It is all but empty . . . I am sorry to have to say . . . I doubt there will be very much water this afternoon . . . or tonight . . . we'll measure what little there is. I drag from brambles the measure pole and she slips the long notched ruler through her hands down and down till we hear a splash and the stick bumps the tank bottom. I lie down and look in and she says . . . Is Mister Echo at home . . .

I call . . . Whoo-hoo . . . whoo-hoo . . . are you . . . are you . . . are you . . . and below we hear . . . You-ou-oo . . . you-ou-oo.

My father comes home and says . . . Damned reservoir . . . you be careful. You're a bit too damned quick to offer the neighbours more than their fair share of water . . . I don't trust old Gaussen not to siphon off more than his due . . . the Abell brothers are a different kettle of fish altogether . . . they at least turn up at church to say thank you to the Almighty on Sunday mornings . . . if you do smell a rat . . . don't hang about . . . jump to it and telephone me . . . I can nearly always be found . . . I'll get on the blower like a shot and soon sort out the old devil.

In wintertime water troughs freeze and my mother says . . . Dress up warm and we will ride and break the ice. It's not right for the young cattle and the ponies to go

thirsty. I'll take a blowtorch with us in case a ballcock is frozen stiff.

The chestnut mare slips on the icy yard slope. My pony pulls at the snaffle bit and edges onto a grass strip and sidles by the gatepost. I hoist my leg and put my heel on the saddle pommel and say . . . You are a clever boy . . . keeping off the ice.

My mother says . . . No flies on him . . . he knows how to look after himself . . . he's like a bear in his winter coat . . . it must be warm as toast inside . . . I'd like his coat on cold milking mornings . . . and I say . . . I wish

I had a bear coat like yours . . . and she says . . . Some nice things had to happen after wartime ended . . . it was a very hard time.

The Valley grass sparkles and I say . . . Can we trot . . . my toes are frozen . . . and the Welsh pony herd gallop at us and shake forelocks and manes and snort. At the old stone trough in the ground my mother leans down and cracks thin ice with a bamboo riding stick and I say . . . The spring isn't even frozen.

My mother says . . . You will find in really cold weather the Valley is always the place to find water.

At Needlehole I hold the mare. My mother hits the ice on an iron trough and says . . . Frozen solid . . . if I burn holes in the ice we should get some-where. Black Aberdeen Angus cattle crowd in a  semicircle blowing steam. She takes the blowtorch out of a saddlebag and twists the paraffin catch open and puts the torch down and lights a match. The flame blasts out short straight and yellow and I say . . . It is hot . . . and my mother says . . . I ought to wear leather gloves . . . let's hope it does the job quickly . . . I don't want my fingers burnt.

She grips the handle in both hands and points the flame and a frilly ice hole opens and turns pale green and my mother says . . . We're through . . . I'll burn two more . . . that way we should be able to lift out a section . . . I hope this is the best way to set a ballcock free . . . when we get back I must ask Joe . . . I need him later this afternoon for ferreting in any case.

Between the coal shed oak and the walnut tree Joe and my mother and I stretch a net over rabbit warren holes and Joe knocks pegs in frozen ground to hold the net. My mother pulls on a leather glove and puts her hand in a hinged flap on a wooden box and says . . . Now you be good Miss Ferret . . . no tricks . . . that's my girl . . . and she pulls out a scarlet-eyed yellowy white ferret. The ferret wriggles and twists and bites her thumb and she says . . . No you don't . . . you behave . . . save your teeth for a bunny rabbit . . . in you go . . . and the ferret runs under the netting and disappears down a hole. She says . . . Thank you Joe . . . I'm all right on my own now . . .

this may be quick or it may take time . . . will you carry on feeding calves and pigs . . . thank you.

We kneel by the net and she says . . . I can't hear a thing . . . can you

. . . she can't have gone off on her own yet . . . if we lose her that will be two gone west . . . is that her . . . here they come . . . don't let her escape. A grey rabbit dashes out of a hole and what looks like white rope follows. My mother's hands grab the rabbit through the net and miss and she runs forward on all fours and pounces and says . . . Got you . . . mister bunny . . . that was simple . . . now don't let's make any mistakes . . . quick . . . bring me the stick. She kneels on the net to hold the rabbit by the neck and smash its head. The rabbit kicks and lies still and she says . . . Very good . . . pull the net back . . . careful . . . that ferret is waiting to escape. I lift netting and the rabbit jumps up and hops out and my mother says . . . Naughty mister bunny rabbit . . . you were only pretending . . . and she lifts the body up in both hands and holds the back legs in one hand and says . . . Give me that stick again. The rabbit hangs and wriggles and my mother whacks the head twice and says . . . Bring the sack . . . better safe than sorry . . . a bunny can get a new lease of life and be off like a shot when you're not looking . . . put the pegs back in . . . good . . . now for that ferret . . . she's gone down again . . . sshh . . . put your ear to the ground . . . is she getting nearer . . . or heading further off . . .

Indoors she sharpens a knife on a stone and slits a line along the rabbit's stomach and hind legs and peels. Skin hisses. The rabbit is cut into five pieces and stews slowly in the bottom oven with carrots.

My father comes home and says . . . God knows how you two exist . . . all rabbit tastes like cotton wool to me . . . any wild duck coming into Fishpond . . . I'll walk up with a gun . . . do my damnedest to shoot a decent meal for all to enjoy . . . followed by a mere soupçon of port . . . I myself shall approach the Coburn '49 at a decanter . . . and he sings . . . You are my heart's delight . . .

6

—————

PATRICK

Once a month my mother fetches her brother Patrick out
from St Andrew's Hospital Asylum to Granny's house for
the afternoon and Patrick follows her into the drawing
room. It is December and I sit in a corner of the sofa and
grip the cat. Granny gives quick small smiles and says
to Patrick . . . Bo darling . . . you do look thin . . . will you
have a biscuit . . . and holds a Crown Derby china plate of
digestives towards him. Patrick sits in the wing chair and
turns his face away and pinches his trousers on the knees.
Granny takes a white handkerchief out of the pocket of
her grey tweed suit and dabs her eyes and says . . . Would
you like me to read today's paper to you darling . . . I
dare say I've put my reading glasses down upstairs . . .
and leaves the room.

My mother says . . . Patrick is going to sit in here . . .
aren't you Bo . . . and I am going to put the car away . . .

there's a hard frost . . . it might not start if it stays outside . . . you come out too and you can carry cookers
in from the apple shed and take them to the scullery . . .
bring a basket . . . don't come back in here without
me . . . not at all . . . you understand?

Apples are spread across slatted racks on newspaper.
Big green pock-marked cookers and small red eaters. I
carry the basket round the back of Granny's thatched
house on an icy brick path and kick a gap in the
evergreen box hedge and step up on a drain in front of
a window and spy on Patrick. He sits and rocks from
his hips in the grandfather Georgian Irish wing chair
that is covered in faded khaki flock fleurs-de-lis. The big
chair is in Indian army photographs of Granny and
Grandfather Hubert's dining room in Bangalore where
five tiger skins stretched out flat are pinned to the walls
so tiger heads snarl down at their dining table.

I watch Patrick sitting in front of a print of a fox-
hunting man in a black top hat and a red coat on a grey

horse falling off an Irish bank into a ditch and mouth through the window to him . . . Hello . . . hel-lo Patrick . . . say something . . . say . . . hel-lo . . . how are you . . . I put my hands together and pray . . . Jesus . . . make him talk to me.

My mother carries Christmas holly past Patrick to the drawing room. I duck and take the apples indoors. Then I run stamping halfway up the thick green-red-blue Indian wool stair carpet and tiptoe back down and into the drawing room and kneel behind the dark-green velvet button sofa while she puts holly sprigs behind picture frames and talks to Patrick . . . Now, Bo . . . we'll all have a quiet lunch together . . . I don't want you to upset yourself . . . this is a busy time for me . . . I have to drive back to the farm this afternoon . . . I'm going out to fetch more holly . . . will you stay here or come? Patrick stares at his black lace-up shoes and my mother leaves. I look over the sofa and whisper . . . Patrick . . . if you talk to me I promise I won't tell a soul . . . why won't you talk . . . I'm going to make you . . . look . . . I lie on my back and wave my feet above the sofa. I crawl and peep round the end and miaow and bark and moo and creep across the carpet towards him and growl and look at his face and say . . . I can make you . . . I can you know. He rocks and stares at his shoes. I stand up and speak to his short black hair and hunched shoulders and say . . . Hurry up . . . I won't tell . . . I swear.

My mother looks in the drawing-room door and sees me and says . . . I told you not to go in there when he's on his own . . . I mean it . . . come on out . . . and don't do it again . . . sit on the stairs where I can watch you.

On the stairs half-landing are Granny's big heavy picture books. I open *The Great War* on my knees. A galloping gun carriage tips sideways at full pelt and a horse screams through open teeth. Another horse lies on its side in water and two horses gallop off pulling reins and harness and a broken centre shaft and a soldier staggers along a wet muddy track. Another soldier kneels and two soldiers lie dead and I think maybe one

of them is Grandpa Hubert . . . I go upstairs and look at
Granny's photographs in silver frames on her dressing
table and I put on her diamond rings and her pearl
choker necklace.

At lunchtime an egg sandwich is put in front of Patrick
on a plate and we have Irish stew. Granny says . . . Bo
darling . . . eat nicely . . . will you . . . show us how you
can. Patrick crams the sandwich in his mouth with both
hands and gets up and walks out of the dining room.
His arms hang straight down and the palms face out and
his knuckles knock against his legs. His white shirt collar
is loose round his neck and his grey jacket is wider than
his shoulders. He goes into the drawing room and we
hear something fall. My mother says . . . You two stay
here . . . I'll fetch Bo.

Granny says to me . . . Is your little pony behaving

nicely, darling . . . I expect you ride him every day . . . oh here comes Bo back again.

My mother holds Patrick's hand and he sits down. She stands beside him. He tips his chair back and I sing . . . There are ten green bottles . . . and change it to . . . There are fourteen dining-room chairs . . . standing on the carpet . . . if one old chair should accidentally fall . . . there'll be thirteen chairs . . .

My mother says . . . That's enough. I hum and sing the numbers.

Granny says . . . The old chairs were made in Ireland a long time ago . . . they will belong to you one day . . . after they are mummy Puss-Cat's.

Patrick takes a sandwich and walks back and forth round the far end of the dining-room table dragging the fingers of one hand along the polished rim. The table is an oval with two long half-moon flaps. Granny says . . . Bo likes the coffin table . . . don't you, Bo . . . it was carved all from one tree . . . at Springhill . . . your daddy's home in Northern Ireland . . . more than two hundred years ago.

My mother twists hair off my forehead and slides in a kirby grip and says . . . It's time for your rest . . . up you go . . . say goodbye to Patrick . . . when I've taken him back you can get up . . . then we'll have tea with Granny and set off for home.

My mother's old bedroom is cold and I curl up in my yellow jersey and Black Watch kilt and white knee socks under a green Indian paisley eiderdown and hear my mother below the window say . . . Come along, Bo . . . I'd like you to be good . . . don't make me have to get cross . . . come on . . . just one more step . . . and Granny says . . . Puss-Cat darling . . . Bo-Dog can stay longer if he wants to . . . and my mother says . . . I'm sorry . . . I have to get back to the farm animals.

I look out of the window and under a thatch fringe I see my mother hold a packet of digestive biscuits out to Patrick from inside the car and hear her say . . . That is a good Bo . . . very good . . . in the front seat . . . you come.

On the drive home I say to her . . . Why doesn't Patrick talk . . . what's the matter with him . . . why does he have to live in hospital?

She says . . . He may have been dropped on his head by his Indian nanny . . . his Ayah . . . on the way home from India in the ship . . . when he was a baby . . . no one really knows.

I say . . . Did he go to school . . . and she says . . . Oh yes . . . he was sent away from Ireland to school when he was six . . . he went to a boarding prep school in England . . . and then to Rugby . . . a famous public school . . . then he went to Oxford University.

. . . Did he talk all that time . . . when did he stop?

. . . He was a very shy little boy . . . he didn't like it when people came to see us at Fernhill . . . he used to hide in cupboards . . . I had to find him . . . and get him to come out. He used to get very cross with me in school holidays. He let my tame foxy escape on purpose. He disappeared the week after he took his final Oxford exams. The army and police searched for him and they found him in a wood on Exmoor. After that he didn't speak ever again. It's sad for Granny but she believes it is God's will. I think people at a place called the Hellfire Club outside Oxford at High Wycombe had a lot to do with it.

. . . What did they do?

. . . They did all kinds of peculiar things . . . look . . . rabbit eyes in the headlights . . . don't they shine.

I stay at home one time when my mother goes to Granny's to take Patrick out. At bedtime she isn't back. It gets dark and I can see lights beyond the granary up in the new cottage past the tractor shed. I go out into the empty summer yard. An owl hoots in Fishpond and I breathe in the garlicky scent of fox and walk along the Barn shadow to the henhouse door. Chinese geese scatter and honk. I chase the geese inside and shut the henhouse bent wire hook.

What happened when Patrick was a boy? I picture him edging down a dark passage at Fernhill sliding each foot and crimping his toes for cockroaches and going into his sister's room his teeth chattering . . . Puss-Cat I'm a cold Bo-Dog . . . I can't stop . . . I can't stop . . . and he stares at the moonlight in the trees and the moon's face and says . . . I hate everyone . . . She puts a blanket cloak round him and his chattering slows down.

He is sent to England in a school uniform that scratches his skin. The buttonholes are small and tight. He is slow doing up the buttons. His sister May 'Puss-Cat' stays behind at Fernhill with Granny Darley and the maids. In the big garden she finds ladybirds to keep in matchboxes and save from wrens. Blue dragonflies crowd on a log that sticks out over the black lake. She wades round the island in case Patrick has come back and is hiding. She gets a letter from him: *Dear Puss-Cat, We all play cricket. I am not very good. I will get better. Tell Mummy to send me a knife and stamps. Your very loving brother. Bo-Dog.*

At the farm on my mother's dressing table is a photograph in an oval silver frame of a small boy and girl sticking their legs out side by side on

a terraced lawn in front of French windows. My mother
says . . . That's Fernhill . . . you can't quite see the giant
redwood trees . . . or the view over Dublin Bay . . . or the
Sugarloaf Mountain behind the house.

I wait for her to drive home from Granny's and curl up
in an armchair and sleep until the spaniel barks at the
drawing-room door. It is getting light.

She has an accident when her car hits a black bull
on a narrow road near Guiting Power. She drives into
the bull head-on and breaks his front legs. She gets
out of the car and kneels by him, and her hands feel
his broken bones as he tries to stand up and falls. She
sits on the tarmac and rests his heavy head in her lap and
she strokes and strokes his face and says . . . I'm sorry . . .
I'm so sorry . . . in the dark I didn't see you . . . why were

you in the road ... where were you coming from at nearly midnight? Try to lie still my darling. Before long someone will find us. Sooner or later the pain will go. She sings ... There is a green hill far away ... without a city wall ... where our dear Lord was crucified ... he died to save us all ... She sings ... The mountains of Mourne ... reach down to the sea ... and ... if you were the only boy in the world and I was the only girl ...

Just before sunrise a milk lorry stops and the driver stands over her and says ... Those Yanks do him ... all over the shop they are ... going like the clappers.

My mother says ... No ... I did ... I saw him too late ... will you go to a telephone box and dial the Hunt Kennels ... Andoversford 248 ... they'll be up and about ... tell them where I am and tell them to send a winch lorry and a kennelman with a gun.

The milkman says ... You'll be half dead of cold ... and my mother says ... He keeps me warm ... be as quick as you can.

The kennel lorry arrives and the kennelman in black rubber boots and a brown overall says ... You can slip out from under him ... then I'll get to work.

My mother says ... I'll stay put where I am ... he's been through a lot tonight ... he's very brave.

The hunt kennelman says ... He's carrying a

mountain of flesh . . . and kneels and puts the gun to the bull's black curly-haired forehead.

My mother says . . . May his spirit for ever rest in peace . . . for the sake of the Father and the Son and the Holy Ghost.

The gun fires and the kennelman says . . . I'll lift his head . . . out you come . . . you going far?

She says . . . Only another seven miles . . . I thought at first he must be Zeus . . . he was a god and a black bull.

The kennelman says . . . Master will be pleased . . . hounds can live off his flesh for a week.

After Granny dies my mother moves Patrick to Coney Hill Mental Hospital near Gloucester so he is nearer to the farm. Four years later Patrick breaks a kneecap and I say . . . What happened . . . how did he do it . . . a kneecap is a thick bone.

She says . . . I don't really know . . . they tell me he banged his knee hard on a table. Six months later he breaks his other kneecap. When the bone heals Patrick walks out of Coney Hill on a stormy evening through the main gates left open by mistake. He is lost all the rainy night and found crouched by a garden shed in a Gloucester garden. He dies of pneumonia. At his funeral are only my mother and I and the vicar and the undertakers who carry his coffin. Next day my mother drives eighty miles from Gloucester to Kilsby across-country and I sit beside her with a box of Patrick's ashes on my knees. She says . . . Granny will like to have him in the churchyard at Kilsby beside her.

7

NIGHT

My father sleepwalks after wartime. Sometimes he stands at the top of the second flight of stairs and shouts ... This place is dark as sin ... bring me some light ... before I break my bloody neck ... get a move on will you ... jump to it.

One winter's night when he's away I sleep in my mother's room and I wake up and she's not there. I walk sideways down the stairs in light from her bedroom paraffin stove. In the dark study my fingers touch sofa chintz and cold curtain velvet. Under the door to the dining room light shows. My mother is asleep with her head and arms on the polished mahogany table and on PAYE columns next to her farm wage book and cattle feed lists and the yellow cover of the *Farmers Weekly* beside a brass paraffin lamp.

I stand on the grey-and-pink Persian rug close to her in my blue Viyella nightdress. Her chilblains bulge by her gold wedding ring and on the other hand by her blue sapphire and red ruby and green emerald eternity rings. A pearl-and-diamond circle is pinned on the turndown collar of her long-sleeved turquoise and pale-brown tweed dress. I pull out a wood pencil between her thumb and fingers and she wakes up. Before she sees me she says . . . Oh Lord.

On winter afternoons she kneels in front of a paraffin stove in each bedroom. She tips back the turquoise chimney and her silver curved nail scissors snip a black burnt wick circle down to thick clean white woven thread. She unscrews a two-gallon can and pours paraffin pink as gums into a tin funnel. The liquid slips into the stove stomach and she says . . . I do wish paraffin didn't reek. She strikes a match to light the wick and a yellow flame circles and meets. Then she twists the silver penny knob so the yellow dwindles to blue. She rights the chimney and sits back on her heels and looks in the little oval Bakelite window to see flame rhythms. Then she bends and sweeps up black fuzzy clippings.

At my bedtime she says . . . Time for this little pony to trot upstairs . . . and clicks her tongue. I prance in front of her. In my bedroom she kneels on the red-blue-green Indian wool carpet and unfastens four brown jersey buttons on my shoulder. I trot on the spot. She says . . . Keep still pony.

I turn my toes in and walk away from her on a blue line by the green wool carpet fringe and say . . . Pigeon toes . . . look . . . and she says . . . Very good . . . a good pigeon . . . will the pigeon come quickly and take off its socks?

I squat on my heels and say . . . This is how a pigeon sits . . . isn't it . . . isn't it . . . and she says . . . Clever pigeon . . . now please can miss pigeon turn back into a pony. I get on all fours and trot on the spot. She holds a cupped palm under my chin and says . . . Here pony . . . nice grass . . . and I turn and kick her hand. She says . . . Naughty pony . . . that wasn't nice . . . do as I say . . . and she takes a handful of my hair and pulls and says . . . Stand up on your hind legs. I pull away and canter across the room and she catches my arm and slaps my legs and says . . . Stand still . . . stand still.

We are silent. She tugs off my Fair Isle jersey and un-buckles my kilt and rolls off socks and pulls down knickers and unbuttons a yellow Viyella shirt and peels up an off-white Chilprufe vest. A red flannel nightdress is on a chair to warm by the paraffin stove and she scrunches up the flannel. I push my arms into long sleeves and poke out my head and get into bed.

My mother sits on my bed and her hands close in a prayer grip. She prays aloud ... Defend oh Lord, this Thy child ... with Thy heavenly grace ... from all the terrors and evils of this night ... for Jesus Christ our Lord's sake ... amen. She strokes my hair and whispers ... Be a good girl and go to sleep ... remember who will come and take you for a ride ... if you lie very still. She kisses my forehead.

Pegasus ... I say after she's gone. Paraffin stove flames flicker up through a circle of holes in the top like gold wasps on the ceiling. My throat is tight and burns. I hold Uncle Alec's Christmas card of a ship on fire at sea and pick at the wall behind my bed with the cardboard corner. The ceiling above me comes down low. I can't breathe. I scratch my palms.

One winter snowy night I hear the stepladder unfold on the landing and my mother climbs up and shuffles overhead in the roof and she calls ... Are you awake ... come up here ... quick as you can ... put slippers on ... come and help ... hurry.

Up in the roof snow is cold and sweet. A hurricane lantern hangs on a nail. She says ... Be very careful ... come towards me ... only walk on beams ... take this bucketful back down the ladder . . . tip the snow in the bath . . . come straight back up.

I say . . . I'd like to sleep up here.

Her shadow flies up the roof. In lantern light her face grows long. She sticks her coal shovel in snow and puts one hand on her hip and one up on a high beam and says . . . Maybe paraffin fumes are worse for you than cold is.

It is a slippery walk along snowy beams. She fills a bucket. I go to her and lean over a tie-beam and touch her fingers and take the handle and go backwards to the trapdoor hole and step down onto the ladder. I go backwards down and walk down the stairs to the bathroom and tip out a bucket of snow. My shoulder aches. I climb back up and say . . . Do you have to take it all . . . and she says . . . If I don't the ceiling will give.

Her shadow slides across rafters and the big dark body bends and straightens. A snow bolster runs between her legs and plump snow pillows lean on walls. I say . . . Look . . . there's a snow cat . . . and she turns half bent and says . . . Where . . . I point and say . . . There . . . and a penguin . . . sitting by a pussy cat . . . and she laughs and digs at the bolster.

I want snow in my mouth. A wind gust wraps cold across my face and snow slides in on my tongue. Snow is the airiness I long for on nights my breathing hurts. Cold tickles under my red flannel nightdress and cools my hot skin. I reach for my mother's fingers and the next bucket and start backwards to the trapdoor.

Snow in the bath melts to dirty brown peaks and ridges. I fall through the ceiling before we're finished. One slipper slips sideways and my balance goes and a leg waves. I straighten up. The bucket weight pulls me over. I stand on one leg on snow over plaster and lathes and put my other foot down like walking on water and go down through the ceiling straight as a soldier and say . . . Jesus . . . Jesus.

It's an easy fall. Lathes snap and plaster crumbles and I hug the bucket and land standing up and my arms let go. The bucket rolls down the stairs and spills white snow on plum-red carpet and I stumble onto my knees in white dust flying and lumps of smashed plaster.

Down the passage the spare bedroom door opens and the dust swirls round my grandmother. She carries her tray of night-time biscuits and her cup for hot milk with brandy. Dust sprinkles her hand-painted violet china and speckles her black hair and she says . . . Good night darling . . . have a very nice sleep . . . and her soft quavery voice stops.

I stand up and say . . . Shall I take your tray Granny? A foxhunt titled in gold letters 'The One that Got Away' is painted on the tray. My grandmother's fingers grip the galloping brass fox tray handles and she stares at me from her dusty spectacles. I say . . . We are clearing snow out of the roof and I fell through.

She says . . . Did you darling . . . that is good of you . . . and she goes back into her room with her tray.

My mother looks down through the trapdoor and says . . . Are you all right . . . don't cry . . . it's not far to fall . . . we're nearly finished . . . and I say . . . I'm not . . . Granny woke up . . . snow is all down the stairs . . . and my mother says . . . How ghostly you look . . . hand me up the empty bucket . . . the carpet won't matter . . . snow is water . . . find a thick blanket to cover the hole . . . open the landing ottoman and look for the grey wolf fur . . . that'll keep the cold in up here . . . get four big books for the corners . . . look in Granny's room . . . the blue and gold *Ancient and Modern* with music is in there . . . and a big picture book of war . . . or the old heavy Bible . . . and fetch your *Fairy Stories* . . .

In the spare room Granny stands in her high-necked long-sleeved lavender nightdress with her back to the walnut cupboard and holds up her silver hand mirror with 'Eva' in Hubert's handwriting on the back in a heart of roses. Her other hand holds her matching silver hairbrush.

When Granny comes to stay at the farm and my father is home he pours brandy into her night-time hot milk and says ... A soupçon of Mr Hennessey's finest, Auntie Eva ... and she holds out the cup to him and turns away and says ... Too many good things ... and he keeps pouring from a cut-glass decanter. My mother always measures out Granny's brandy  in a silver spoon with 'Over Fork Over' engraved on the handle on a banner floating under an upright unicorn chased by an upright lion.

The first April after wartime my mother and father drive in the open Bentley across Europe to Nuremberg through the Swiss mountains and wildflowers. I stay with Granny at her thatched Hunting Lodge in Kilsby.

One night she slowly brushes my hair and says ... Darling ... did you know it was our ancestor who saved King Arthur of the Round Table ... poor King  Arthur had to escape from his enemy so he ran through a hayfield where our ancestor was building a haycock and said ... Quick ... hide me under the hay ... Our ancestor forked hay over

King Arthur and the enemy ran by. King Arthur came out from under the hay and said to our ancestor ... Thank you very much for your help ... your family motto shall be Over Fork Over for ever and ever ... So that's why our family plates and spoons and forks and the big silver tray say 'Over Fork Over'. That is a nice story isn't it. Now kneel down and say your prayers darling.

Lately I read a history of the Lenox-Conynghams' seventeenth-century Ulster home called Springhill and the haycock story is recorded in the book but this time King Macduff is running away from bad Macbeth. Our ancestor is still making his haycock and hides Macduff so Macbeth runs on by. Then Macduff comes out from the haycock and says to our ancestor ... Thank you very much for your help ... your family motto shall be Over Fork Over for ever and ever ... Anyway whatever the story there are silver forks and spoons and snuff boxes and a tray engraved 'Over Fork Over' thanks to the farmer who was making hay.

After wartime a man often visits the farm called Stephen Peel. Very occasionally he brings his wife Rosemary. My father is at home for one of their visits and afterwards he says to my mother ... Keep an eye on that joker ... he's making one hell of a show of being a country gent . . . though I don't anticipate much of a way forward with that wife.

Stephen comes often when my father is away in embassies in Europe. Walking up the yard beside my mother and me he says . . . This place could do with proper investment . . . how many acres do you farm in toto?

My mother says . . . Two thousand . . . altogether . . . that includes woodland and I plan to let out three hundred. My mother and I chuck henfood out of a speckled enamel bowl and the hens run behind our navy-blue summer canvas shoes. Stephen says . . . I'll take a look at the farm account figures gratis any day of the week.

My mother does not allow him into the cowshed. She says . . . It is Milk Marketing Board regulations Stephen. I do not want to upset them. TB has done for a whole herd at Prestbury . . . not far from you . . . we have every inch disinfected. She ties her hair in a green-and-red paisley pattern scarf she hangs off a pipe in the dairy and pulls the heavy green doors on rollers shut to a crack and says . . . I shall be some time, Stephen . . . please do not wait.

I sit on the feed bin lid and watch him look up the yard and button three gold blazer buttons and get into his polished car. When Rosemary comes she wears high heels and a black-and-white houndstooth tweed pencil skirt and a pink blouse with a bow. Her hair is two long plaits pinned up round her head. She says . . . I could never learn to milk a cow . . . even if I starved.

Stephen sets fire to Rosemary while she is asleep and after the murder he goes missing. I hear landgirls in the kitchen say . . . A murderer . . . could be he's hiding up here somewhere . . . she might look out for him . . . she never would . . . I reckon he was sweet on her . . . I'm not sleeping under this roof then . . . the postman says they say they found poor Mrs Peel's jewels in the ashes of her bed.

The hunt for Stephen comes to the farm and policemen in blue uniforms look over stable doors and climb high wooden ladders onto hayricks in barns and walk up Homefield to Fishpond Wood.

At Seven Springs Girls' School the two headmistresses nicknamed Haddock and Willy-B stand beside me at going home. My mother drives the green van up the corkscrew drive past beds of red and pink tea roses and waves to me. Haddock says . . . We won't see you at school tomorrow . . . not until . . . off you run . . . be very careful.

Mrs Fish and her lovely auburn-haired daughter Betty walk over from Needlehole after the police are gone. In our kitchen Mrs Fish says . . . He's a man . . . he gets hungry . . . stands to reason . . . I saw carrots went missing this morning and he was out there this afternoon . . . before we came over I put a loaf out on the table . . . and a quid . . . the door's not closed. I said to Betty . . . We'll be off now . . . he'll know . . . he'll be back and take the bread . . . the quid'll tell him he's in good luck . . . he won't go far . . . You can telephone and tell the police to come on back this way . . . that way Betty and I can get a ride home.

At bedtime my mother says . . . Stephen has been safely found . . . he hid in the woods by Needlehole and a nice police dog followed his scent. He will stay in prison now . . . he will not come and see us ever again. It's a very sad story. We'll say Our Father especially for him . . . and for Rosemary. We pray . . . Our Father . . . which are in heaven . . . hallowed be Thy name . . .

The next day I get dropped off at the red gate after school and start running home. A tree shadow lies across the drive and I see Stephen Peel hiding in the branches. I climb over the iron railing fence and run round the sunny side of the tree and climb back and run past Triangle Field and up Sheep Dip hump. I stop at the green corrugated-iron tractor shed. Something moves behind a tractor wheel. I crouch and liquid drips off an axle rod. I touch the rod and sniff my fingers for blood. Above the cart shed in the dark granary I hear noises. I go up the outside stone steps and climb across hundredweight sacks of barley and oats and pinch sack shoulders and climb back out. I run down the yard and ask my mother . . . Did Stephen come and see you after he set light to Rosemary . . . and she says . . . Not that I know of . . . our new kittens might be born any minute . . . run and fetch a cardboard box from the coal shed and get ready a soft bed.

That night I lie in bed and shut my eyes and watch what Stephen does. He unscrews a paraffin lamp glass chimney and lays it on the bedside table. He twists the filler cap that jerks on a safety chain and pours pink paraffin on the blue eiderdown and the pillows near Rosemary's long brown hair she has unplaited. He puts the lamp down quietly and lights a match and touches the flame to wet paraffin stains. Yellow flame trickles along blue satin eiderdown and fiery blue and yellow grow and burn. I see Stephen run like the wind. Rosemary lies in the flames. My mother looks in my bedroom door and says . . . Are you asleep?

My father comes home and says . . . Damned lucky the bloody man didn't take on my old Mrs Fish . . . that's one blessing. Set your own wife's bed on fire . . . God Almighty . . . I ask you. I don't want swashbuckling types around my lovely home . . . not ever again. I warned you the so-and-so was making a show of being a country gent . . . bastard was a hundred per cent on the make.

Next time you mark my words. And a damned socialist to boot. Ernie Bevin and Co. have plenty to answer for . . . yes siree. He sings . . . Lord . . . lettest now Thy servant's soul depart in peace . . .

On fine-weather mornings when milking is done my mother and I ride to my school. She leaves me at the Seven Springs crossroads and says . . . Be very careful coming home on your own. If a car is in sight at this crossroads . . . wait . . . ride over only when the Cheltenham–Cirencester road is all clear and watch out for big lorries coming from Gloucester round the bend.

After lessons I saddle up in the school stables and cross the road and trot up the gulley beside Chatcombe Wood. One day there are gypsy caravans. I see washing on hazel bushes and grazing ponies roped to shafts. Then men in black trousers and braces and dark shirts with no collars walk out and spread arms wide open and make a fence across the grass track. One catches my pony's reins down by the snaffle rings and another grabs the saddle flap either side of my leg and one stands in front of my pony smiling and his gold tooth shows. He says . . . You'll like a bigger pony . . . you can take our grey . . . leave your little fellow behind . . . I look at the grey pony's scratched knees and crooked hocks and I say . . . My-daddy-is-a-policeman-and-he-is-at-home-off-duty-today . . . The gypsies laugh and let go of my pony. A woman says . . . You tell us what your daddy tells you to my darling . . . that's the way. They slap the pony's backside and he gallops up Chatcombe Hill.

The next day my mother finds hoofprints on our land near Chatcombe Wood and my father says . . . Bloody gyppos . . . grazing damned ponies at night . . . our best grass seed ruined . . . worth its bloody weight in gold. I'll damned well show them a thing or two. They think they can trick an old colonel . . . they've got another think coming. I'll tell you that for free . . . yes siree.

After tea he spreads newspaper across his desk and takes apart one of his matching pair of Charles Hollis twelve-bore guns and teases a wad of tow onto a brass rosewood rod and rams the rod down the barrels. He unscrews the rod into three sections that lie in a green-velvet-lined gun case. He rubs an oiled lambswool rag on steel curling feather scrolls and on the barrels and on his engraved initials and on a cross-hatched arrowhead and a safety lock thumb ledge.

My mother folds back the two halves of the walnut card table and takes a red leather box out of the table drawer and says . . . Gold or green? I say . . . Gold this time . . . I'm going to win. We shuffle two packs of Evening on the Nile playing cards and lay out Racing Demon on green baize. My mother says . . . Ready . . . steady . . . go . . . and we slam down cards and play until dark falls.

Out in the starlit yard we get into the jeep front bench seat. My father drives into Homefield and through the Rushys. He turns off the car lights at Ratshill. At Dewpond sliprails he stops and says . . . Out you both get . . . keep close to Dewpond Spinney and follow the Chatcombe track . . . fan out in the seed field . . . that knife will slice through hobbles like butter . . . got the necessary halters . . . good show . . . gyppo ponies are used to being led . . . ride one and lead two . . . any more will follow on . . . leave the sliprails open . . . I shall drive to the main road and wait at Chatcombe corner . . . if any gyppo action starts up I can intercept . . . if all goes according to plan I shall be home safely before you.

The bullfinch fence we walk beside is black and I hold my mother's hand. She whispers . . . Listen carefully for ponies munching . . . there's one . . . listen . . . over to the left . . . keep close . . . look.

We go up to a piebald grazing. My mother pulls his forelock up and lifts his head and pushes his nose into a webbed halter. She bends and cuts the hobble rope and says . . . Let's put you up on top sweetheart . . . up you go . . . you wait here. She swishes away in wet grass and comes back with two ponies and hands me halter ropes and whispers . . . When I come past you follow . . . keep out of moonlight if you can.

The piebald's back is warm and damp. A skewbald

walks either side and a loose skewbald follows. I listen to my mother's three ponies' hoofbeats on Chatcombe grass track and Ratshill stony ground, and then squelching on Rushy bog and then breaking ruts in Homefield gate and scattering yard stones. The owl hoots in Fishpond Wood and I hear my father say . . . A first-class operation all round . . . well done the cavalry.

He stands outside Big Barn door and his gun barrel pokes down across his arm. His cigarette end burns and the black-and-white spaniel shivers by his feet. He says . . . In you go . . . remove all halters . . . don't want the so-and-sos making off with our possessions when they turn up . . . which they will do in due course. Plus I intend to make things as difficult for them as I can.

Piebald and skewbald ponies puff and pull at hay in the barn. My father closes the two big black doors and

locks a padlock and says . . . I rather think a soupçon of Mr Cockburn's first-class young port is in order before bed . . . do I have the permission of you two sporting ladies . . . may I invite you to join me . . . we'll have taught the gyppos a thing or two . . . that's worth a small celebration. He sings . . . If you were the only girl in the world and I was the only boy . . . and we go indoors.

In the night the marmalade cat jumps off my blue paisley-pattern eiderdown and crosses the Indian carpet and leaps up onto the window-sill between the flowered linen curtains. Then he steps out of the window and slides straight down the house face clawing at stone. If I look out of the window I see bats and a cat that looks black heading for Big Barn.

Morning light colours my flowered curtains and my father is shouting in the yard . . . You bloody gypsies . . . let this be a lesson to you . . . leave my land alone . . . do you hear me . . . if I find your damned ponies in my seed field again . . . I'll shoot the bloody lot. You're lucky to get off scot-free this time. I can tell you that. Next time will be an entirely different story ... you mark my words.

From my window I see the skewbald and piebald ponies trot up the yard ridden bareback by four gypsy boys and two men. My father slams the front door and comes upstairs. He and I go into my mother's room and he says ... That should teach them a lesson ... my best guess is they won't venture back here again. There will be one hell of a price to pay if they do ... I should say. Now for a short period of shut-eye before breakfast ... hush-a-bye everyone ... and he sighs.

My mother says ... I'll be seeing the gypsies at Stow Fair as usual I expect. That's why they camp at Chatcombe ... they always come this way. They usually bring us up clothes pegs ... I must ask Mrs Fish if she has enough this spring.

8

BLESSINGS

In the 1930s between the two world wars the Pytchley foxhounds become a favourite of Edward, the Prince of Wales, and attract la crème de la crème of English hunting society. Captain Peach Borwick is a Pytchley Master and four days a week Cecily gallops close as she dares across the shires behind her husband Peach.

One day Cecily boards the Rugby train to London and takes a taxi to St James's Piccadilly. In high-heeled brown lizard shoes and a tweed suit and pearls and a green felt cloche hat and brown kid gloves she walks from Locke the royal hatters to Peels the royal bootmakers and along to Fortnum and Mason. She is measured for a top hat and for handmade hunting boots. Then she buys crocodile shoes and a handbag and silk petticoats and knickers and

The Pytchley Hounds WILL MEET ON		
MONDAY	Nov. 22	FOXHALL INN
TUESDAY	,, 23	
WEDNESDAY..	,, 24	CRICK
THURSDAY	,, 25	
FRIDAY	,, 26	MARSTON TRUSSELL HALL
SATURDAY	,, 27	WELFORD

Each Day at 10.45 a.m.   STANLEY BARKER,
Please see all secure.   HUNTSMAN.

J. STEVENSON HOLT, NEWLAND, NORTHAMPTON.

brassieres. She buys a silk shirt for Peach at Turnbull and Asser in Jermyn Street and lunches at Overton's Fish Restaurant on Dublin Bay prawns. Her cousin May joins her and they compare days hunting and horses and polo ponies and dances and discuss boyfriends for May and the three other girl cousins.

I am guessing at Cecily's day in London. My mother tells me what happens when Cecily gets home. My mother is Cecily's cousin May.

Cecily walks in the oak front door and in the hall are Peach's muddy boots and spurs and his pink coat with a white Pytchley collar. He is home and after a day's hunting Peach and Cecily always share cocktails upstairs in their big white chilly bathroom while they take turns in the hot bath water. Their favourite cocktail is a White

Lady. Dry gin and Cointreau and lemon in equal parts shaken feverishly with ice. Today Cecily looks in the dining room and sees the silver cocktail shaker engraved with their intertwined initials is on the sideboard beside the silver ice bucket. She mixes the cocktail and carries the shaker and two pretty conical glasses upstairs.

Peach is out of the hot bath. He sits in a white wicker chair reading *With Rod and Gun through the Western Highlands*. His wavy brown hair is slicked down and his shiny shaved legs are crossed and his skin is pink and warm and he wears Cecily's cream satin whalebone corset threaded with pale-blue velvet ribbons.

Cecily says . . . Oh, you sweet darling . . . you've saved the hot for me . . . did you kill . . . I'm dying to hear . . . London was a bit damned dreary . . . I swear it. Peach keeps on reading and Cecily puts the two cocktail glasses down on the marble washstand by a Chinese willow pattern china bowl. She unscrews the shaker and pours and holds out a glass. Peach takes the glass and pouts a kiss and sips and says . . . Tell you when you're in . . . gallop or the hot'll be cold.

I say to my mother . . . Is he really wearing her corset . . . isn't she shocked rigid . . .

My mother says . . . Not in the slightest . . . we all know about Peach . . . he'd been asking us for our cast-off brassieres for years before he and Cecily were married.

1932

DATE	HOUNDS	MEET	TIME	HORSES	
26ᵗʰ Oct	Pytchley	N. Kilworth	9.0	Woodstock (Bay tree)	
Nov: 2ⁿᵈ	Pytchley	Watford Corert	10.0	Woodstock (Bay tree)	

FROM THE PYTCHLEY COUNTRY.

The Pytchley, in common with neighbouring packs, have finished a really good and a really satisfactory cubhunting season. The going had been perfect, scent has served well, the young hounds have entered well (I should say extraordinarily well), and both packs have accounted for a number of foxes. What has been a particularly pleasing feature of this season's cubhunting is the way in which the hounds have caught foxes in the more difficult places, and some of them are extremely difficult.

REMARKS

Drove out to S. Kilworth - Lots of foxes
K. House 1 killed. At Kilworth sticks for
ages 1 little ring round 3 fields + back
to sticks - Then a jumping hunt in
right hand circle to N. Kilworth village
+ hounds hunted on to K. House.

Lovely — much the best day so far. Rode
out. Fox ran 2 fields + back to Cover. Away
again swung out over W. Haddon brick rd with
lots of jumps back across rd + on slower to
green lane gravel pit holes!! From brick ran
quite well to a drain nr Yelvertoft (fun) bolted
+ eat him. Woodstock a lovely boy.

11 Days Cubhunting. &9 Woodstock
1 Fall   1 Crystal
Rode astride   1 Grey Pony
                     (6 Bay Tree)

She didn't take a blind bit of notice. She only told me because I'd said to her in London that June and I were going to join the FANYs and she should too. She rabbited on to Peach about what I'd said as soon as she was in his hot bath. And she was still telling me joining up was the silliest thing and she'd never do it after wartime was in full swing.

Out hunting Cecily wears a black silk top hat and criss-cross bumblebee net veil down over her dark eyes. A Melton cloth dark-blue tailored jacket slopes beautifully across the line of her hips onto the ankle-length skirt that folds and falls to the heel of a black leather boot. A little polished wheel spur shines as she gallops across ancient grass. Her horse leaps open-ditch cut-and-laid fences and crashes through bullfinches and soars up over the river below Althorpe Gorse. She leans well back and slips the reins through her gloved fingers right to the small polished buckle and her pigskin and chrome flask of Singing Johnny clipped to her saddle bumps her horse's ribs.

A special train steams into Barby village station and transports hunt servants and hunt horses and grooms and the pack of foxhounds to the distant meets. Hunt servants twirl and crack whitened plaited leather hunting whip lashes. Grooms in black leggings and jackets and breeches lead the first horses off the train and mount

and jog a mile or so to someone's big country house. Chauffeurs park Rolls Bentleys and Lagondas on raked gravel beside clipped mown grass drive verges. Astrakhans and wolf fur coats are taken off and thrown back inside the cars. A groom leads up a horse and the rider in breeches and boots or a side-saddle skirt hops on one foot. The groom cups his hand and gives a leg-up and throws the rider into the saddle. Horses' manes are plaited into a row of knots sewn up with needle and thread in the early mornings. A butler and footmen in black trousers and jackets carry silver salvers among the horses and hounds and offer up little cut-glass tumblers of dark-red port. Ivory and tortoiseshell and silver and gold cigarette cases flick open and are held out from on horseback. Fingers in yellow string gloves stuff cigarettes in amber and ebony and ivory cigarette holders. Grooms walk away down the road to the train and lead out second horses and mount and jog behind the hunt at a distance. If a first horse has a bad fall or goes lame or sweats up tired a groom canters along. Horses are swopped over and the groom walks the first horse back to the train and waits for the end of the day's hunting.

The Saturday Pytchley Field of roughly eighty riders wear pink or black or navy-blue coats and top hats and bowlers and velvet hunting caps on fresh corn-fed clipped-out half-thoroughbred horses. During a twenty-minute wait for a Saturday fox to be found in a cover the twisted-leather saddle girths are yanked up a hole or two tighter and horses fidget. Double-bridle curb chains chink and hooves stamp and riders' knees bump and stirrup irons clang . . . Stand still will you . . . I say watch out . . . damn you . . . time for a gasper . . . will you stand damned well still . . . lucky that frost lifted . . . things didn't look too certain early . . . May rides black dock-tailed Gobo. Her cousins Cecily and June and Mary and Tinker are out. The five Anglo-Irish horsy girls christened 'The Blessings' by subalterns.

. . . Good morning, Birdie . . . morning Vi . . . how goes it . . . Doggo . . . nasty frost yesterday . . . frightened the hell out of me . . . vastly afraid today'd be called off . . . Pug . . . how's that leg . . . Babe tells me you're having it off . . . giving it one last outing are you . . . good man . . .

I'd do the same . . . look out . . . here comes Scrummy . . . old trout is riding astride . . . I'd think twice before showing off that backside . . . perfect day . . . Scrummy, what say . . . top class . . . may be one to remember . . . if we're lucky . . . my God, Chalky White is in a sorry state . . . Bambi saw Lilah head off in Chalky's motor late last night . . . poor old Bambi, that'll get him down . . . Kitten's coming this way . . . I'll take off sharpish . . . I see Piggy's following her . . . that's a damn good arrangement . . . Ducky said Piggy's put Daphne in the family way . . . my dear fellow . . . good morning to you . . . I'll make you an offer for that liver chestnut . . . not a chance in hell, old boy . . . think I'll say good morning to Piggy . . . Blessings look ready for the fray . . . June . . . Cecily . . . Mary . . . May . . . Tinker . . . good morning to you.

The five Irish girl cousins grow up sharing a governess

and playing hockey and polo and Sardines and Racing
Demon and Ludo in large houses. June's and Cecily's and
Tinker's father is Pat Miller and he keeps a stable of polo
ponies for hire. His telegram address is Polo England. A
few miles up the dead-straight Roman Watling Street
is the Weedon Cavalry Officers' Equestrian Training
School where soldiers learn to ride. Weedon provides
young cavalry officers galore for horsy girls to dance and
flirt and play games with.

The Blessings compete in
polo matches in summertime.
Polo ponies with hogged manes
and plaited tails knotted up so
as not to tangle with swinging
polo sticks are trotted by grooms
riding one and leading three to
Rugby station. In the train the
grooms twist hay wisps and
rub at horses' muscles. At a big
house in the English countryside maids lug copper coal
buckets upstairs to bedrooms to heat baths for weekend
house party guests. Girl grooms in fawn jodhpurs and
white Aertex shirts stand holding fresh ponies ready for
the next chukka under clumps of green shady trees.
Officers offer girls with bobbed hair Turkish cigarettes in
slim silver and gold cases and inside the lid are engraved

handwritten scrawls about love. ... Frisky Girl ... passionate yours ... Bestyest.

The cousins all fall in love with horsy men. Cecily marries Peach Borwick the Pytchley Hunt Master. June marries Dermot McCalmont, Master of the Kilkenny

foxhounds in Ireland. Mary marries Chicken Walford and after Chicken is killed in battle she marries Frizz Fowler who becomes Master of the Meath hounds also in Ireland. Tinker the youngest cousin wants to marry Captain Bertie Bingley who is an English cavalry officer and international polo player. May has horsy boy-friends and one bookish one at New College at Oxford who longs to marry her. He is a socialist and wants to be a writer and sends her letters lecturing her against the conservative capitalist values of her army beaux.

The eldest Blessing is my mother's cousin June who wakes early one summer morning before maids bring up jugs of hot water and before fried liver and bacon and scrambled and poached eggs are put out on the dining-room mahogany sideboard under silver lids in silver dishes kept warm on a steel hotplate over nightlight candles. She pulls on jodhpurs and tucks in an ironed white cotton shirt and brushes her black bob-cut hair in a swinging shield mahogany dressing-table mirror with a blue malachite silver-rimmed hairbrush. She walks down the curving polished staircase in her fawn cotton ankle socks and into the dining room to pick up sugar lumps out of a silver bowl to give to polo ponies and some cheese biscuits out of the silver biscuit box for her to munch and she sees her father rolled up in the Afghan rug on the polished oak dining-room floorboards dead.

I ask my mother . . . Why is he rolled up in a rug . . .

My mother says . . . We think to muffle the noise of the gun when he pulled the trigger . . . he had the rifle in with him . . . friends out hunting said he was a great deal changed after he'd come back from France and the war . . . he fought in the trenches on the Somme . . . not far away from where your grandfather Hubert was at the end.

Between the two world wars 30,000 men are treated

for shell-shock in England and hundreds of thousands more keep stories to themselves and endure nightmares and anger and tears and deafness and days when their legs let them down and they are ill to the stomach and are suddenly sick. My grandfather Hubert told my grandmother Eva it was as if the whole world shook over there in France.

The government allocate one million allotments to returning wounded non-commissioned soldiers and war widows. A small patch of land to plant carrots and parsnips and Brussels sprouts and cabbages and potatoes and onions in winter. And in summer broad beans and French beans and peas and radishes and parsley and lettuces and marrows and rhubarb.

At the farm my mother learns from Mrs Griff that Griff fought as a soldier in the First World War. Their son Tom is killed early on in World War Two. She takes vegetables and sewing to Mrs Griff in her cottage next to Kilkenny Cross Hands pub opposite the Foxcote turn. A photograph of Tom Griffin in uniform is on the brick mantelpiece in the small dark downstairs room. A coal fire smokes and burns in a small black grate most of the year round.

Mrs Griff is small and plump and her white hair is rolled in a thick grey hairnet. My mother sits opposite her in Griff's low brown armchair. I sit on the stuffed arm. My mother says . . . There's a dozen hens' and four ducks' eggs. Joe will leave cabbage and sprouts.

Mrs Griff says . . . I was saying to Griff . . . if I'd had your hens and the ducks when he was off in France . . . things might've been different . . . and when that war was over as well . . . there were people starving then . . . and they died . . . you didn't tell anybody if you went hungry . . . you had your pride . . . I wouldn't have told anybody if I was hungry . . . all your budget went on food . . . there wasn't money for medicine . . . the doctor stood outside the house with his bicycle . . . he wouldn't go in . . . not to a woman in labour . . . not till he had a shilling . . . we collected up and down the houses. On a baby's death certificate they wrote . . . consumption of the bowels . . . that was what they called starvation. Babies so frail they had to be carried on a cushion. The allotments did come in handy . . . there wasn't enough though . . . not for everyone . . . we wanted food distribution . . . not all that malnutrition . . . children just lay there and died . . . it was pitiful . . . quite a lot of children died . . . it really upset me . . . that this country let the children have all that pain and did nothing . . . after two million volunteered.

My mother says . . . Thank goodness Griff came back . . . I heard one in eight widows died within a year after they lost a husband.

Mrs Griff says . . . What could they feed children

on . . . fresh air . . . you can't feed them on fresh air . . . I took children in . . . five children . . . they were crying so before she died . . . 'You can't go, Mam . . . we all love you so much.' She says to me . . . 'You'll look to them . . .' What was I to do . . . two died at ours . . . I used up my coal . . . I kept them warm . . . that was the thing I did . . . I'm glad of that. Griff was with horses . . . lovely horses he said . . . Boxer and Duke and Violet . . . he never saw them again of course . . . when tanks came along. He says it was very terrible . . . tanks mowing through the wounded . . . I tell him it wasn't any better here . . . food went where the money was . . . bread was black . . . you couldn't get white bread . . . we didn't want another after Tom . . . not after seeing those things. I say to Griff . . . 'Don't go down the allotment . . . there's the things off the farm . . .' It's better for him that way . . . I don't go down . . . don't like to. Here's your petticoat I stitched . . . silk is murder . . . slippery . . . like always . . . her jumper will be ready Sunday . . . when you fetch me to church.

I say . . . Thank you very much for knitting it for me Mrs Griff.

My mother says . . . Off we go . . . up you get . . . say goodbye to Mrs Griff.

Outside I say . . . Why does Mrs Griff talk to you all the time.

My mother says ... Men don't talk much ... particularly the ones that fought.

The night before cousin June gets married to Major Dermot McCalmont in the big church in Daventry my mother sits on June's bed and June says ... D'you know what happens ... I haven't got a clue ... Mary told me it hurts dreadfully ... she won't tell what ... she says it's as bad as galloping downhill side-saddle ... is it really ...

I say to my mother ... What did you tell June ... and my mother says ... I told her it's all foreign news to me ... I'll make Cecily tell in the morning ... she has got to pass it on ... she is the only one who's married. Then Cecily wouldn't tell unless June gave her Auntie's gold fox pin ... Cecily was always impos-sible ... anyway Cecily does tell June on her wedding morning ...

... It's a riot June ... you'll love every minute ... from the very first night Peach says I'm to bring upstairs a hunting crop ... and my top hat ... and have not a stitch on ... I just ride him astride ... he's like a narrow little mare galloping along in a point-to-point ... the winning-post comes when he shouts out ... I'm there ...

I'm there . . . you're the darlingest bestest Blessing in the whole wide world . . . he is always most delighted and I am none the worse for wear.

I say to my mother . . . Does June believe Cecily? . . .

She says . . . Yes . . . I bet her a day's hunting on The Lark that Dermot will be exactly the same . . . I knew June would like that . . . I never let her ride The Lark. I told her . . . You are fit as a flea June . . . you'll come to no harm . . . why would you . . . you'll have a lovely big house . . . and an absolute ton of hot water. It will be gorgeous.

June and Dermot marry and live in Mount Juliet in County Kilkenny in Ireland on the banks of the River King and the River Nore that flow with trout and salmon. The house has many bedrooms and drawing rooms and a billiard room and a squash court and a tennis court. The Tetrach was a famous thoroughbred stallion winner of all seven classic races he ran in and stood at stud at Mount Juliet in the First World War. Champion jockey and six times Derby winner Steve Donoghue said that the weird elephant-grey horse blotched all over with brown splodges was the nearest thing to a bullet in animal shape he ever rode. The Tetrach sired 135 foals and eighty were race winners. I see his grandson Mister Jinks standing at stud in The Tetrach's same grand stable at Mount Juliet.

My mother lifts me up to see Mister Jinks through the bars on his oak door. The horse is grey and blotched dirty as if filthy soapsuds have been chucked at him. His neck is an arc of fat. I say to my mother . . . What's he pawing the stable floor for? . . .

She says . . . He's a stallion . . . he gets impatient waiting for his next wife.

Between the two world wars May spends part of each year in Ireland at her grandmother's Edwardian white-turreted house outside Dublin. Fernhill has a famous garden with giant redwood trees and a view over Dublin Bay and the Sugarloaf Mountain behind. She loves Fernhill but she misses the other Blessings to play games with. Patrick her brother goes for long walks on his own. Tinker is the youngest Blessing and May's dearest friend who writes letters about English dances and polo games and hunting and who's kissing who and when and where. In August 1936 a telegram comes to Fernhill for May saying . . . *Puss-Cat, please come home, your Tinker.*

Tinker is ill and un-happy. She lies in bed on

white Irish linen pillows in a house in the Pytchley country. Her mother, Olivia, stands by the bed and says ... I repeat Tinker. You are not to marry Bertie Bingley ... no Tinker ... not on any account ... I know a great deal more of your Captain Bingley's history than you do ... you are absolutely forbidden. Anyone would think no other officers exist. Weedon provides you with hordes of young men who know how to waltz and play a decent game of polo ... which are Bertie's only decent qualifications. I would like to know for a start what you have against Frizz and Jaff and Bill Boville ... really Tinker ... pull yourself together ... you are not in the slightest ill ... I am not calling out Doctor Evans and that is that ... do you understand ...

Before May arrives Tinker dies.

I say to my mother ... Did Tinker really and truly die of a broken heart ...

My mother says ... I don't properly know. I couldn't catch the night boat. I would have done anything to have been back in time. Doctor Evans told Auntie Olivia afterwards that Tinker had appendicitis. Your granny told me that she was over at the house the day before and Tinker said to her ... Tell Mummy I've promised Bertie I shall marry him ... the divorce isn't his fault at all. The funeral was awful. All I could think about was who will ride Pesky now ... no Tinker to hunt Pesky ... we've all got our own horses ... Tinker won't like Pesky being sold. Afterwards Auntie gave me Pesky and I lent him to Bertie. I knew Tinker would be pleased. Poor Auntie didn't notice. Pesky made quite a decent regimental polo pony ... not up to international standards. Then wartime came and after we were married we brought Pesky to the farm. He lived for three more years. He liked it best in the Valley.

Bertie Bingley's mother is Mrs Noel Bingley, maiden name Roëll, has two baby sons at Tikki Mooni tea estate on the island of Java in 1902 and 1904. Mrs Bingley is Dutch. She and Mr Bingley invite out family and friends who arrive by ship to stay and write merry rhymes about the fun they've had in a Visitors' Book. But upper-class English boys must go to public school in England. Tikki Mooni is sold. A fortune is made. The Bingley family return to England and rent lovely medieval Notley Abbey by a stream between Thame and Aylesbury in Buckinghamshire. A polo ground and a grass tennis court are measured out and mown and rolled. The boys grow up. Bertie loves house parties. Waltzing. Hunting. Croquet. Girls. Then the 1929 Wall Street crash ruins London City investment houses and Mr Noel Bingley is made bankrupt and dies. Notley Abbey goes. Mrs Bingley rents a small house in the country town of Devizes.

Bertie is a subaltern in the Eleventh Hussars cavalry regiment . . . Prince Albert's Own . . . the Cherry Pickers . . . dress uniform crimson and gold. A subaltern's pay is too small for the expensive life and so he becomes dependent for income on his brother officers' charity. Not a happy situation. He marries a pretty girl nicknamed The Brat.

The regiment are posted to Afghanistan and officers shoot ibex in the Khyber Pass and Bertie grows a red beard. He says . . . Bloody wogs think I'm descended from the prophet Mohammed . . . apparently the fellow had a red beard . . . they come running to me to settle their disputes . . . I ask you . . . The regiment goes to Egypt and Bertie is shipped home with suspected tuberculosis with his wife. They rent a country house and one feverish night he wakes alone in bed and comes downstairs to see where The Brat is and the green-and-gold brocade dining-room curtains sway. He pulls the curtains back and she is making love with the family stockbroker on the matching brocade window seat. Anyway that's the story he tells and says . . . With a bloody tradesman . . . I ask you . . . if she had had an eye for a brother officer . . . the whole damned future would be altogether different . . . dear God . . . what else could I do? He cites the stockbroker and divorces her and does not support his son and daughter. He sends the children Christmas cards and presents after wartime and when he marries my mother she remembers their birthdays. They occasionally come to the farm.

When Bertie and Alec arrive in England to be sent away from their parents to school aged five and seven they start stammering. Bertie's stammer starts up again if he is nervous all his life.

The first time I travel to London by train with my mother is to see my father receive a war medal from King George VI in Buckingham Palace. The King has a stammer. My mother and I wear hats and best coats and very polished shoes. We walk along red carpets and sit in rows of blue-velvet chairs with gold-painted legs. My father appears from behind a crimson curtain and bows to the King. The King hangs the coloured medal ribbon round his neck and they have a long conversation. After the ceremony I tell him . . . Daddy . . . you talked to the King much longer than anyone else . . . and my father says . . . Y-yes b-b-but n-n-neither of us s-s-said a w-w-w-word . . . off we g-go t-to the C-Cavalry C-Club for a s-slap-up l-l-lunch. My mother says . . . I didn't think of that . . . two stammerers together . . . my poor Bear . . . and the poor King.

Between the two world wars after Tinker dies May travels to Kenya to visit cousins. She sails onto Sri Lanka – then Ceylon – and more cousins. She is away for four months and when she comes home there's a letter . . . *Have you returned from your wanderings . . . it's no fun with you away . . . all my love, BB.*

Two of The Blessings, May and June, are FANYs. They strip down transport lorry engines and march in straight lines in khaki serge uniforms.

Bertie Bingley lives in the Inns of Court barracks at Sandhurst and May's FANY HQ is at Camberley just up the road. They all go to the cinema and play billiards and polo and ride in point-to-points and hunt, and May and Bertie fall in love and get married on 21 December 1940. They live in barracks until the farm is bought in August 1941.

I think they first fall in love out of pity for each other. Tinker is such a terrible loss. Bertie's bride to be. May's best friend and they belong to the same tribe and play the same games brilliantly well. May rides like an angel with hands of silk. In the Pytchley Country it is said . . . If you put May Lenox-Conyngham up on a horse its value doubles before it leaves the stable yard. He plays regimental and international polo and hires ponies from May's Uncle Pat at Polo England. They talk the same language: napkin and passage and loo and what . . . Never say serviette or corridor or toilet or pardon. They wear their tribal colours in tweed and cavalry twill and camel hair and linen and silk and velvet and cotton. With brogues. Never a nylon mac or coloured slacks or a dress with shiny gold buttons or co-respondent shoes. They go to church. They'll always have money. Or . . . she will

because she will inherit part of Fernhill from her grandmother. And there is something else. She writes in her
diary . . . Oh B, my darling . . . a wonderful evening . . . I
can't believe I am happy.

They march and gallop and laugh and dance cheek
to cheek at the Berkeley in Knightsbridge to Victor
Sylvester's orchestra. After one evening he motors his
Lagonda south to his Tidworth barracks in the sunrise.
He says . . . There I was bowling along enjoying Mother
Nature at her very best . . . next thing a godforsaken
racket starts above my head and a white curtain hangs
before my eyes . . . and a voice whom I presume to be
St Peter calls to me in a damned fury . . . Jesus bloody
Christ . . . my Christ . . . come on out here . . . get out
here bloody quick . . . come on . . . give me a bloody
hand . . .

I admit I am damned surprised at St Peter's choice of
English . . . from his throne at the gates to heaven and
hell . . . which is where I suppose I am . . . hey-ho . . . I
step out to discover my old Lagonda has left the damned
road and parked herself halfway up a bank of spring
flowers . . . and what is more I see a lorry load of iron
milk churns rolling and banging over her roof and milk
pouring like billy-ho all over the shop.

I climb out and the lorry driver gets down from his cab
and says . . . Thought you'd met your Maker then did

you my son ... let's get to work ... I've got a delivery due for this.

We collect up churns and push the old Lagonda off the bank. Before he goes on the driver takes a look at my black bow tie and silk shirt and dinner jacket and says ... Out dancing were you last night ... you think about marrying her ... spend the nights at home and less harm done ...

He was a damned nice fellow which is why I took his advice.

After wartime The Blessings come over from Ireland for the Cheltenham Gold Cup Race Meeting in March. Every year my mother says to my father ... We'll put the Irish silver out ... and he says ... You are asking for trouble ... as you wish ... forge ahead ... no belly-aching if the aftermath is what I predict ... agree ...

My mother canters her chestnut mare up Homefield and my father says to me ... We'll simply carry on as per my original plan ... it will only cause one hell of a dose of misery if we don't and then my story turns out right.

In the house I walk ahead of him and hand him silver. Point-to-point steeplechase challenge cups, cups won in gymkhanas, at polo matches, working-hunter show classes, best turned-out pony, Welsh mountain mare and foal, pony stallion, driving pony, Connemara breeding-mare, hunter trials and children's showjumping. I pick up handfuls of spoons and forks: teaspoons, sauce ladles, an Irish viola-neck eighteenth-century soup ladle, salt cellars, jam pots, napkin rings. Silver foxes, pheasants, racehorses, wild ducks, candlesticks. Cigarette boxes, ashtrays and pens and inkwells, silver writing pads and matchboxes. A miniature stool blue-velvet pincushion on cabriole legs garlanded with silver roses. A Russian samovar. A big oval tray engraved with signatures scrawled by my father's regimental brother officers. A mirror framed in tiny furious silver men in battle tunics and brimmed hats holding hands. My father holds a hessian corn sack open in one hand and puts the silver in.

We carry two full sack loads up the yard to the henhouse. He swings both by the necks in under a row of nesting boxes on stilts and says ... Out you go ... no hanging about ... fresh air is in order ... no self-respecting burglar ventures inside a henhouse ... bloody awful stupid creatures hens ... frightful stinkers ... beyond any words. Who would have thought the Almighty in His wisdom would create a blessed miracle – the egg – from such a bloody stupid creature as a hen. I sometimes wonder if St Peter will be standing at the gates of heaven holding a plate of perfectly scrambled eggs on buttered toast as a welcome ... only time will tell. Shall we reward ourselves for a small act of sabotage successfully conducted with a sumptuous mixture of Mr Bournville's chocolate powder lightly stirred into the beloved Baroness's fresh milk . . . what say . . .

The silver is stolen from my mother's house on Cheltenham Gold Cup Race afternoon years later. My father is dead but I can hear him say . . . Silly old Bear . . . damned hoi polloi.

After wartime he takes a box at Cheltenham Races in the new Queen Mother stands. Looking over the balcony from our top level I see down into the members' enclosure on black bowler hats and brown trilbys. Silk headscarves decorated with horseshoes and horses' heads and whips. Slanted velvet berets. Behind me my mother unfolds brown greaseproof paper in a tartan tin and lifts out a rich fruit cake biscuit crisp on the outside with a slightly mushy centre. My father says . . . How about a slice of the famous snipe-bog cake before ravening hordes find their way up here and the fun begins . . . plus a soupçon of port . . . to deter the cold . . . a little more than a soupçon for a colonel who fought the war.

He says . . . I see on the race card a half-brother to the Lion of Judah is running in the two-thirty steeplechase. Shall I throw caution to the winds and risk our lovely home . . . if the horse comes in first at twenty-to-one that solves the pothole issue at a stroke . . . we'll have the entire drive tarmacked in a jiffy . . . we all know the Lion can damned well jump . . . hey-ho . . . better be a good boy . . . must be sensible and keep a roof safely over our heads . . . *è pericoloso sporgerse* . . .

My mother says to me . . . Are you ready to go down . . . pull up your socks . . . put on your gloves . . . and remember cousin June has a runner over from Mount Juliet . . . Frizz and Mary say not to put a sixpence on . . . Mary always says June is the richest Blessing and too mean to give her horses enough to eat . . . I'm sure that isn't true.

My father says . . . May I make it quite clear that in the future . . . if I come across any broken-down Irish race-horses abandoned by your cousins eating their heads off in our Valley . . . I shall turn the damned things loose on the main road. Are we ready to venture down . . . leave the door open wide . . . you will find that the presence of Her Majesty Queen Elizabeth the Queen Mother in her own box two floors directly beneath will ensure that only a certain kind of person will be permitted up this staircase.

Before the last race my mother says . . . If we head for home now we'll avoid the awful car park traffic jam.

My father says . . . First-rate idea . . . make a smart getaway . . . the hoi polloi clog up every road from here to Seven Springs. I shall steer the Daimler past the mighty British police force on the gates ... once safely through I shall let the uninebriated younger generation take over the steering wheel. That said you and I can safely finish up this excellent port.

My mother says ... There are bound to be police on the lookout in Cheltenham ... if an under-age driver is caught it is the car owner who loses a licence.

My father says ... To hell with bloody rules and regulations ... if my daughter can hunt a racehorse across Cotswold country and is not allowed to drive my first-class Daimler on a tarmac road I say what the hell did we win the war for ... don't play windy buggers with me ... step on it ... let's get a move on ... or our own beloved horses will get their tea late.

9

HUNTING

My chestnut pony and I gallop at a Cotswold drystone wall beside Tiger Blaney on her young bay horse. My pony takes off and rises over the wall plus a hidden barbed wire oxer an arm's length from the far side. I see the pony's ears go back and feel his hind backside shove off the ground and hear his tail whisk as he sees the wire. I grab a fistful of his mane and look down and he flies into a grass field.

Tiger's horse's legs catch in wire. The horse leaps and hops and pulls. Fencing stakes nailed to wire break and bump along the grass. The frantic horse kicks and Tiger half steps off and half falls and lets go the reins. The horse struggles in a circle and pulls barbed wire tight round Tiger. She stands like a circus ringmaster and

screams. Her hands grasp at sharp barbed knots. Her dark-blue jacket tears. She shouts . . . Get wire cutters . . . get wire cutters . . . and I say . . . Jesus.

I stand up in my stirrups and look across the fields. A whipper-in in a scarlet coat trots past three elm trees two fields away. I turn the pony and whack his ribs with a hunting crop and race at the wall back the way I came and jump where the wire's pulled off. I stand up high in the stirrups and yell . . . Wire cutter . . . wire cutter . . . and gallop and yell. He gallops towards me and I scream . . . Over the wall . . . wire . . . wire . . . this way . . . after me.

He jumps back into Tiger's field behind me and pulls up and unbuckles the flap on a leather pouch clipped on his saddle. He pulls out cutters and springs off and runs and snips wire between Tiger's horse and the wall. Tiger is dragged on the ground. The whipper-in runs beside her body and snips wire that ties her to the horse and she lies on the grass. The horse hops away and his legs bleed. Other people gallop up and kneel by Tiger and call out ... Someone find a car ... look for a hurdle ... where's there a road ... are we nearer to Cheltenham or Cirencester hospital? I shout ... Cheltenham is six miles from here and Cirencester is eleven. The whipper-in walks over, takes his horse's reins from me and mounts and says ... Well done ... I'm going on.

My mother says ... You must always *always* look out for trouble on the far side of a fence.

My father says ... The pony must have jumped a damned near perfect parabola to achieve that height and distance ... you'll have told him to stand right back at take-off ... it's imperative always to keep an arc in mind ... that way you reach the height and don't fall in the ditch ... or on the damned barbed wire. Barbarians using that stuff ought to be banned from farming in hunting country. That's the colonel's view ... not worth the paper it is written on mind you.

I like hunting foxes with ginger biscuits in my tweed jacket pockets. My chestnut pony champs at the chrome knotted snaffle and twisted pelham barley-sugar bar on his tongue and the hooked curb chain rattles. Thin saddle-soaped leather reins run from his bridle mouthpiece to my hands. My new double-bridle is a Christmas present and my mother says . . . When you ride in a double apply the bottom rein with care . . . wrists nicely rounded . . . pretend you've got pennies balanced on your thumbs . . . the curb chain and pelham bar act as a vice on his lower jaw . . . never pull with your arms . . . that way you ruin a horse's mouth and he won't go nicely for you again . . . ever . . . unless you've got all the time in the world to set things right . . . he's been hurt and learnt not to trust you . . . that's a big lesson to undo . . . even if you're being run away with pulling at a horse's mouth won't do any good and it's unkind . . . in a runaway situation steer round in a circle on one rein.

A hard frost sets in. The ground is cold. Scent does not lie and hunting is cancelled. My mother says . . . I'm driving into Chelt . . . if you change out of trousers into a skirt you can come.

I say . . . I'll stay at home.

Two stair flights above my room and through two empty bedrooms is a square door into the attic. I crawl in and swipe my jersey sleeve across steamer trunk labels: Bangalore, Darjeeling, Dar es Salaam, Nairobi, Java, Argentina, Dublin, London . . . Batavia Shipping Lines. I stand up under the sloped ceiling and my head bumps on a pork leg hanging up to cure.

Our farm pigs are named after kings and queens or princes and princesses. My father carves cold ham at Sunday supper and says . . . Remind me . . . am I about to enjoy a delicate slice off Princess Elizabeth's bottom . . . or is it Princess Margaret's . . . I forget . . . not that it makes a damned bit of difference. Hey-ho for the dear old Ministry of Agriculture who pay us handsomely to breed piggy-porkers. Allow me to tempt you to another slice . . . go on . . . be a devil. You have the word of a cavalry officer you will come to no harm.

In the attic I sidle by a running ostrich. Cobwebs over his fat black glass eye stick on my Fair Isle jumper. I open a mahogany box. Inside is a sloped green baize writing desk. I buckle on a red-and-gold belt fastened by a silver coat of arms and put on a hard white topi hat and lug the writing desk by two brass handles over bamboo polo sticks and a pig-sticking spear and black mouse droppings on yellowing tissue paper.

In my bedroom I look inside the portable green baize desk. Visitors' cards and black-edged writing paper and cream envelopes are in compartments underneath the baize. I rub a thumb across embossed crests and addresses. A standing unicorn is chased by a standing lion. A bear's head looks out of a crown. Crusty purple ink flakes off an ivory dip-pen.

My wind-up gramophone is by my bed. I lower the arm and put the diamond needle onto a record's shiny black edge. The needle hisses and slips onto circular grooves and a man's voice recites 'Sounds from the Hunting Field' – side one.

Foxhounds whine and yelp and the hunting horn

wails. The master's voice whoops and yells . . . Seek him . . . seek him . . . whoo-ee . . . aiee-ee . . . where's he . . . where's he . . . and growls . . . Come here . . . come over here . . . come on back little ladies . . . and his voice rises . . . Come on . . . come to me . . . come . . . come away little ladies . . . come away-ee-ee. I listen to hounds until the needle scratches and I lift the silvery arm and turn the record over and get under my blue eiderdown in a knitted yellow polo-neck jumper and thick green corduroys and listen to side two – 'Digging Out and The Kill'.

My blue eiderdown comes from London. My mother arrives home from Andoversford station one summer bedtime and places a creased brown paper parcel criss-crossed in hairy string on my green Witney blanket. We sit and unpick gorgeous knots and scratch at lumps and pull at loops. Whiskery strands loosen and the waxed brown-paper ends lift and the centre flap opens. Our fingers feel inside and my mother says . . . I think we've caught him . . . hold on tight . . . here he comes. A shiny eiderdown puffs out. Rose-pink Indian paisley whirls on sky-blue cotton. She says . . . He's come all the way from Peter Jones in Sloane Square. He'll keep you nice and warm in wintertime. Now . . . into bed and say your prayers.

The next record, 'Hang Out the Washing on the

Siegfried Line' ends on the gramophone and I hear my mother calling ... Are you upstairs ... come down and shut the attic door ... this house is turning to ice ... be quick as you can ... the wireless says this frost is here to stay ... I'm driving a tractor down to feed the Valley ponies ... hurry and get a move on and you can come.

I run upstairs and shut the attic door and run downstairs and pull on boots. I push my arms into a tweed jacket and tug on a knitted red balaclava and red wool gloves and run up the yard. My mother says ... You are dressed-up ... mind out you don't give the ponies a fright ... they'll think you've come from the North Pole ... there's quarter of a sack of oats ... chuck it on the two-wheeler ... then come back for hay.

It thaws and hounds meet at Kilkenny and find a vixen in Lineover Wood. My mother says ... Follow me ... I know where she'll go ... she can't get into Bogden ... Charles stopped the earth last night.

Charles Parker is the Cotswold Hunt terrier man. He walks the countryside night and day carrying a sack and spade. He wears scarlet wool knee socks and cord breeches and muddy lace-up boots. His home is a caravan in his mother's parkland.

My father says ... God alone knows what goes on inside that caravan. I'll bet the place stinks to high heaven. Damn man had a perfectly good public school

education. No good reason why
he has to make up his mind to
live like a bloody gyppo. When
he turns up here late at night
you're to offer him a proper
glass of whisky. After that be
sure to see the joker on his
way. Do I make myself under-
stood?

My mother says ... He
always keeps on the move ... I passed him and a boy by
Needlehole early the other morning ... the wind had got
up at night and I'd ridden over to tie the windmill down
before milking.

The Lineover vixen runs for Bogden Bank and doubles
back to Chatcombe Wood. My mother says ... Come
on ... gallop ... we'll cut across below the windmill.
The fox leaves the Ratshill bullfinch ditch and turns
left-handed past Needlehole for Seven Springs. Master
catches us up and he and my mother and I ride to keep
the pack in sight. I see the small tired fox crossing the
Cheltenham to Cirencester road and turning down-
stream towards Coberley. The lead hounds close on her
and she jumps at ivy on a willow and falls back. Master
steps off his horse to whip off hounds. He folds the wet
bronze fur body over the palm of his left hand. He puts

his copper horn to his mouth with his right hand and blows a long double note . . . killed. He stashes the horn between his second and third polished gold coat buttons engraved CH for Cotswold Hunt and flings the fox on a log and flashes a short knife down on the fox's neck and pads and brush. He chucks the body in the air and shouts out lovingly . . . Good little girls . . . eat it up . . . eat it up . . . good girls . . . good girls. The bitch pack yowl and scramble and tear and bite and turn away and lie down and pant.

Master walks over to my pony. He carries the vixen mask in his left hand and dips a finger on his right hand in her neck. He lifts his arm in his muddy pink coat and draws a cross in warm blood on my two cheeks and on my forehead. He says to me . . . Want this do you . . . and gives me the vixen mask. He says to my mother . . . No baths for her for a week . . . what-what-what . . .

Blood dries and tickles my skin. My pony snorts and people lean down to me off their horses and say . . . Got the mask . . . did you . . . rode well today . . . a mask for you is it . . . congratulations . . . great occasion huh-huh . . . you'll never forget today . . . been blooded have you . . . lucky girl . . . remember well you were Master's bridesmaid.

My mother's chestnut mare sidles towards Master's bay horse and crosses her white stocking front legs and

her rear legs. My mother looks down at me on my pony and the smears on my face and says . . . Aren't you a lucky girl . . . and fox blood on my yellow string gloves seeps into wool linings.

Master says . . . Hounds ran well . . . could have covered the whole pack with a blanket by Needlehole . . . staying out are you . . . I'll draw Abell's side of Hilcot . . . might find Gaussen's dog fox . . . Charles says he lies up in there. Then head for home up your valley if we don't find. Call it a day . . . what d'you say. I'll put a Whip on your valley gate. Keep your ponies in.

My mother says . . . We'll follow on . . . don't know how to say thank you . . . say thank you to Master, sweetheart.

I blink and see mud on my eyelashes and say . . . Thank you very much Master.

Charles Parker says . . . I'll take that off you . . . He

puts the mask in his sack and says to my mother . . . I'll be along tonight.

One hunting season years later the Cotswold meet at the farm and set out to draw Bogden Bank. My mother gallops up Homefield and jumps the Springfield wall by the Airplane gate. The chestnut mare takes off and she and my mother fall down in the pit the water boys dug that morning on the far side of the wall to bring mains water to all our fields.

The horse's body halts and twists and somersaults on top of my mother. Four white legs thrash and kick and the mare rolls sideways and half stands and clambers up the side of the pit. She stands and listens. Her skin quivers and she trots hopping lame towards the whimpering sounds of hounds casting in the wet. The reins swing under her neck and a stirrup iron lies across the saddle. Over by Little Grove someone sees her coming and says . . . That's May's mare . . . try to catch her . . . you bring her on . . . I'll look out for May in that direction. Someone else says . . . Last seen May was headed for Chatcombe.

The water boys are laying down pipeline in Rushy Bank. They hear the echoes as pipes bang and clank and they drive their open truck back up along the Springfield wall and their pipeline ditch. They see my mother and lift her out and lay her on the truck. People gallop up and someone says ... Take my horse ... I'll go with her.

In the yard someone unbuttons her hunting jacket and unpins her gold fox tiepin and unknots her cream silk stock and says ... Look ... she's got a note sewn in her jacket lining ... it says 'Please Do Not Take Me To Cheltenham Hospital'.

My father says ... If those young men had got a proper move-on with their jobs instead of coffee-housing we'd have been fully on the mains last autumn. Then we wouldn't be where we damned well are now.

My mother's skull is cracked in the fall and she is in Cirencester Cottage Hospital for a month. She never hunts again. Medical advice is that another accident could cause paralysis. She suffers spasmodic headaches and double vision. She says when the pain comes it is as if cheese wire cuts across her head.

She starts the Riding for Disabled in the Cotswolds and says to me ... What would be best of all would be a purpose-built riding school on Cheltenham Racecourse that is easily accessible with stables and a couple of fields for ponies ... they say disabled people enjoy the feel of movement on a pony that they don't get anywhere except for swimming ... there's just no knowing how many might like riding from around Gloucestershire. At the beginning she and her friends lead borrowed ponies in Oriel School riding arena in Cheltenham. She fund-raises and enthusiasm grows. Seventeen years later the Disabled Riding School is built and two fields alongside are bought in a corner of Cheltenham Racecourse. By 1994 when she dies 200 disabled riders a week take part and 200 more are on the waiting list.

One cold hunting morning I gallop my bay pony too fast round a hill shoulder on white frosty grass. The pony's legs slide away and he falls. My collarbone snaps and I am taken to Cheltenham Hospital before my mother hears what's happened. A general anaesthetic wears off and I come to alone in a room with no feeling below my knees and start screaming . . . My legs . . . my legs . . .

My mother waiting on a hospital passage bench hears my voice and runs in with a nurse and says . . . It's all right . . . they've left your hunting boots on . . . why on earth do they give you a general anaesthetic . . . it's made your legs swell up . . . that's why you can't feel anything . . . so no one has cut them off . . . they're there . . . I promise you . . . stop screaming . . . it's such a hopeless hospital . . . try to lie quietly . . . we'll have to slice off the boots at this late stage . . . I ask you . . . they behave as if it's wartime in here . . . no one finds time to do things properly.

The brown leather hunting boots were made to measure for my mother when she was a girl and fit me perfectly. A surgeon's knife slices down the seams and my mother says . . . It is a well-known fact that extremities can swell considerably under an anaesthetic . . . is that not in your training? At home she says . . . Well at least you are alive . . . not like poor old Ratty who went in with a broken pelvis and never came out. You'd think things would've improved. I know in the First World War Granny set wounded soldiers' broken bones in Dublin and when I asked her how she knew what to do she told me . . . I just did what I thought was best . . . but for heaven's sake we've had another war since then . . . you'd think things would be done better.

My father says . . . Old Ratty had hands of iron . . . God alone knows how many horses' mouths he ruined. That however is not reason enough to bump a fellow off in bloody hospital. Not in my opinion . . . for what it's worth. He sings . . . Glorious things of Thee are spoken . . .

10

KISS-ME-QUICK

A scarlet Royal Mail post van drives down the yard at lunchtime and my mother says . . . Run . . . there's a telegram.

My father says . . . That man's petrol gets paid for by the poor old bloody taxpayer I'll have you know . . . these socialists are a bunch of thieves if you ask me . . . by the time this Labour government has had its fun the hoi polloi will all own bank accounts. Then you'll see borrowing hit the skies . . . you mark my words.

My mother says . . . In wintertime bicycling up is very cold. She says to me . . . Quickly . . . in the kitchen . . . butter four sandwiches with jam . . . Kiss-Me-Quick and Hug-Me-Tight are on the Fishguard train.

We ride three miles downhill across fields to

Andoversford station and tie up to black iron railings under pines. Waiting we look down the railway lines and eat plum jam sandwiches in greaseproof paper. My mother says . . . Pay attention when the ramp comes down . . . they've been travelling all across Ireland yesterday . . . and on the boat last night . . . and a train today . . . they have every reason to try to escape.

A closed cattle truck is linked on the end of the passenger train. The stationmaster hammers a bolt and runs backwards and a steep ramp falls and bangs the platform. A pale chestnut and a Connemara dun stare out of the dark. The stationmaster climbs up the ramp and claps his hands and the two Irish ponies slide down and jump off the ramp. I catch the chestnut's halter and we lead away. He lifts the ramp and clouts the bolt and blows a silver whistle and waves a green cotton flag. The wheels turn and white smoke hides the pines. The stationmaster's office door bangs. Birds sing. We stroke the two new ponies and feed them apples and handfuls of grass.

My mother says . . . Not a mark . . . what luck . . . we'll go home gently via St Paul's Epistle . . . Hug-Me-Tight might be in foal . . . and hold on carefully . . . Laura says Kiss-Me can be naughty.

We mount and lead an Irish pony each. Past the post office and Jack's garage and the police station and the village school and on uphill to Kilkenny Cross Hands Inn.

We turn left into St Paul's
Epistle Lane. My mother says
... St Paul's letters to the Corin-
thians are buried in the mound
under the trees ... I can't think
how they got here ... but that's
the story.

Out in Sheep Pen Field the
new ponies gallop. On the far
side of Five Acre fence a pony
stallion snorts and trots circles.
He turns and gallops and flies
over the stream and oxer and chases Kiss-Me-Quick and
traps her in fallen ash tree branches. The stallion rears
and comes down forelegs astride her back. Kiss-Me-
Quick shakes her head and walks. He bites her neck.
Looking from the gate they become a two-headed horse.

My mother says . . . If he's put Kiss-Me-Quick in foal it won't be the end of the world . . . her baby can play with Hug-Me-Tight's.

Hug-Me-Tight, the dun Connemara, foals early one morning in springtime. We see the cream foal swaying on long legs. His black nose bumps along under her belly.

 A month later Kiss-Me-Quick paces up and down the stream. I lead her into a stable and talk to her . . . Good girl . . . lovely girl . . . you'll have a beautiful baby . . .

The foal gets half born. My mother pulls at its front legs. Her hands slip. She pulls again and the foal drops onto stable straw. Kiss-Me steps away and stands by the manger and breathes fast. My mother says . . . Let's leave her . . . she'll calm down . . . we'll wait outside and listen.

Her hoof hits brick and my mother says . . . Quick . . . back in. Kiss-Me-Quick has her rump towards the foal. My mother says . . . Kiss-Me . . . Kiss-Me . . . stand back . . . get away . . . leave the foal alone . . . now I say . . . stand still . . . calm down.

I stroke the mare's face. My mother lifts the wobbly foal and his nose nudges his mother's chest. Kiss-Me stamps front feet. She looks down at him and bites his neck and she backs off to a stable corner and kicks the whitewashed brick. My mother says . . . Don't be a beastly mother . . . he's your very own foal . . . he's lovely . . . and she says to me . . . Are you strong enough to hold her . . . don't let go . . . whatever she tries . . . I don't trust her one inch.

Kiss-Me stamps and kicks. The foal falls over and can't stand up. We lift him onto a horse blanket and hold four corners and lug him down the yard into the kitchen and lay the blanket by the open warmer oven door. I rub his fur with a yellow duster and cover his shivery body with a dog-bed blanket. My mother stands on tiptoe to reach over and drags the silver dented kettle onto a hot plate. She adds warm water to cow's milk and stirs in raw egg yolk and honey and quarter fills a cider bottle with the mixture. We stretch a black rubber teat for feeding lambs over the bottle mouth. She shakes drips onto her wrist and says . . . Try and start him on fingers.

The foal lies on his side. I kneel and wriggle a finger on his tongue and lift his head with my other hand and look in his eyes and say . . . Come on foaly. I push three fingers in the back of his throat. He swallows and his tongue rubs my fingertips and he sucks a gentle rhythm.

My mother says . . . Well done . . . and pushes the black teat in beside my fingers and says . . . Now . . . slowly . . . pull your fingers out . . . once he gets going . . .

half the battle's won . . . he has a good fighting chance . . . if he lives till morning.

The foal gets a drink every half-hour the first day and every two hours at night. My mother says at breakfast . . . The kitchen is going to get filthy . . . I'll ask Joe to bring sacks of sawdust down for the floor. We must keep the dining-room door shut or he'll fall down the steps. Beastly Kiss-Me. I shall ask your godmother Laura where her behaviour is inherited from when I write to Coolalta.

Before we go shopping we put a horse rug in the dark-blue Ford V8 Pilot and lift the foal onto the back seat. We fold his legs and lay newspaper under his tail. My mother says . . . I wish the van had not died. She parks in Cheltenham High  Street. I wait with the foal while she buys groceries and picks up machinery parts and saddlery repairs and Virol from Boots the Chemist to put in his milk. The foal dozes with his head upright and his nose on the blanket between his folded knees. If he tries to get up I twist round and tickle his lips with the cider bottle teat.

People stop and look in and say . . . Where's its mother . . . what's its name . . . I'd like it on our couch . . . isn't it messy . . . is it a boy . . . or a girl . . . can you get it out for us . . . go on . . . why's its tail like a brush . . . the fur is lovely . . . is it for sale . . . I look at the foal's face and he looks back at me and sucks.

In the kitchen the foal noses the edge of the table and scampers from Esse to dresser and back. The dining-room door gets left open and he stumbles down three steps and nuzzles mahogany and nudges a silver challenge cup off a plinth. A row of prize silver cups chimes and falls. He runs backwards and his fuzzy tail bumps the rosewood spinette sideboard. Port and whisky and gin and sherry in the decanters slurp. His yellow muck spurts on the grey-and-pink Persian rug and he picks up a silver candlestick in his teeth and shakes his head and flings the candlestick against a wall. I point an empty cider bottle at him and he follows me back and I shut the door and say . . . Be good and stay in the kitchen.

My mother says . . . He will have to learn to live outdoors . . . soon on fine days he can get used to Sheep Pen with the Welshies. We'll feed him a bottle at lunchtime and make him a hurdle and horse-rug bedroom in the top cowshed near the calves so he hears them in the dark. He will see us come and go while it is still light.

In the yard the foal follows my mother or me or Joe or Griff. Mrs Fish pushes past him and claps red soapy hands and yells . . . Get away . . . get off me . . . you dirty thing

... beat it I said ... bugger off ... go on ... you heard me ... and she starts to cough. The foal stops and watches her and turns back to the kitchen door.

Shut in Sheep Pen Field the foal neighs and looks beyond the gate into the corrugated-iron green tractor shed. Joe and Griff wire-brush mould florets off spark plug threads and tip petrol from orange five-gallon army cans into tractor tanks and twist screwcaps tight with oily rags that were white linen sheets and flowered cotton dresses. Munday leans on a front tractor wheel and rolls flimsy papers round Woodbine tobacco wisps. He strikes red-tip England's Glory matches and smokes while the foal calls outside the open double doors.

Oil drips make pools under tractors and Joe and Griff pull Z starter handles from clips inside rear wheel guards. Joe bends over and presses a hand on the blue tractor bonnet. His other hand rattles the handle down three holes under the radiator and plugs a crankshaft rod that pokes from oil-sealed engine casing so the handle locks on. He hauls the engine round. Inside the cylinder head a dry spark plug hit by a rising piston ignites an explosion and pistons jump smartly up and down.

On a good day jumping pistons suck air and petrol mix from carburettor inlet valves that shut tight quick after the suck. On a bad day Joe heaves the bugger of an engine waiting for a spark to ignite and air and petrol to explode. A running tractor engine explosion occurs forty times every minute. In the yard my mother hears a tractor start up and says . . . Good news.

Griff teaches a landgirl to grip the Z handle and turn the four-cylinder engine and heave up till gravity pulls the engine weight and handle down over again and again. The girl stays bent over and carries on. Sparks ignite and the engine coughs and stops.

My mother says to landgirls . . . Always put your thumb and fingers together along one side of a starter handle . . . piston explosions turn the handle round very fast . . . there isn't enough time to let go if your fingers and thumb are together . . . I've heard conchies are forever breaking thumbs . . . you girls are quicker to learn . . . it is a miracle when a tractor starts . . . I say a prayer . . . always.

Joe shoves the handle back in the mudguard clip and stands in front of a tyre tall as himself. He steps his laced brown leather boot up on the muddy brake pedal and reaches for the rusty steering wheel to pull up by and sits on the perforated iron seat. He shoves his left boot on the muddy clutch pedal and slams the gearstick ball handle. The gearbox groans and the foal sees the Fordson Major back out of the tractor shed.

The postman's red van bumps over Sheep Dip hump and freewheels down the yard and the foal calls when the van comes back. My mother looks over Sheep Pen wall trotting by on her chestnut mare. The foal trots alongside and she says . . . Hello foaly . . . are you lonely . . . I know . . . it's very hard being all on your own.

In Bull Pen Beau Brummell the Ayrshire bull rubs horns on pine rail knots and looks at the foal out of five round bars. A cockerel and hens stalk into Rickyard and flap up muck heap sides and scratch wet brown straw on steaming heaps of manure as high as Griff on a trailer can fork muck. Welsh ponies graze by the stream and step over ash twigs and cross the field munching short grass. Thick purple grass patches grow round horse droppings. My mother says . . . We'll keep the foal in the yard for two days and move yearling steers from cattle pens into Sheep Pen and graze it down. The Welshies are making a big mess of the top half. A week after the steers leave my mother and Joe put a dozen sheep in to graze the grass short for summer growth. At lunchtime the telephone rings and Major Jim Gaussen says . . . Hello . . . hello . . . your sheep . . . on the main road . . . I've notified the police . . . goodbye.

Damned sheep . . . my father says when he hears . . . Always will find an exit. The day the Almighty created sheep He was on poor form in my opinion. Lucky the flock didn't cause one hell of a car smash. Don't want us held responsible for God knows who being killed so my Bear is sent away to languish in Gloucester prison. No fun to come back to our lovely home and have to drink an after-dinner glass of our secret Cockburn '27 on my own. No siree. I'd be a hundred per cent for ridding ourselves of the entire flock if I did not fear the consequences. You can bet your bottom dollar a Min. of Ag. johnny will show up sooner or later to check if we are good boys farming our proper quota. Don't want to get in hot water. Hey-ho. No harm done this time . . . better fetch up on our knees on Sunday morning to say thank you to the Almighty. He sings Crimond . . . The Lord is my shepherd . . .

In Sheep Pen on a hot day the Welsh ponies stand nose to tail under larches along Rickyard fence. Tails swish pony faces and flies swarm and land and tails flick and flies swarm all day.

The foal keeps away from the Welshies and stands on his own. I call to him as I come home down the drive

after school. He trots along Sheep Pen wall and sticks his nose over the nailed-up Sheep Dip wicket gate. I climb the wall and walk beside him and his top lip wriggles in my palm. He noses after me through Rickyard gate and follows me down the yard and shoves at my back. I run and swerve and the foal trots. He comes in the kitchen and puts his forehead on my stomach and sighs and I scratch tufts between his ears and give him my fingers to suck.

On a sunny day I sit by Sheep Pen wall and share cow cake with the foal and wait for my mother to come home. His head droops and he breathes on my face and rests his nose on my shoulder. The Welsh ponies graze past and one nudges at my foot and bites the toe of my black rubber boot. The foal's head doesn't move and the Welshies move on across the field to Five Acre oxer fence.

At night the foal cries in Cowshed pen behind horse rugs thrown over the hurdles to keep out draughts. I hear him from my bedroom and go downstairs and cross the yard and sit in a corner of the pen in a yellow checked Viyella nightdress and a blue flannel dressing gown and red felt slippers. The foal nibbles my face and hair and sucks my fingers and bends knees and hocks and folds up. Lying down his breathing slows and I climb out over his hurdles. The foal scrambles to his feet and neighs three rising notes. I climb back in and sit and scratch his neck and pull his soft ears. He sighs and lies down and stretches flat out. I listen to rats shuffle in sackcloth at the empty sack pile and see bats whip across the cowshed double-doorway dark sky and breathe last year's hay and sackcloth dust and cobwebs hung on bricks and cow dung stuck to concrete and horsehair on my dressing gown. The foal's breaths get shallow and slow and I climb out quietly and tiptoe up the shed and over yard stones and go indoors and back to bed.

At breakfast my mother says . . . If you go out at night to foaly you'll only teach him to be sad without you . . . he's got to learn to sleep alone.

I see her chase rats away from empty sacks and cowshed drains in early mornings before milking. She leans back and smacks a wooden bristle broom on the

cowshed cement floor and says . . . I won't . . . have . . .
it . . . I . . . won't.

At bedtime she reads the 'Pied Piper of Hamelin'
poem aloud and I say . . . What happens . . . after the
end . . . the mountain didn't open . . . it couldn't . . .
where do all the children the Pied Piper saves from rats
go . . . where are they living now . . .

She says . . . The Pied Piper took them to his lovely
secret place . . . be a good girl and say your prayers . . .
defend oh Lord this Thy child . . . from all the terrors
and dangers of this night . . . for Our Lord Jesus Christ's
sake . . . amen. She kisses my forehead and turns out the
light and closes the door. Mice run behind my skirting
boards and across my ceiling. I dream rats eat my face
and hands and arms and legs and feet and the foal is
calling me.

One day I run down the yard and the foal trots to
meet me and rears up taller than I am. His front hooves
strike my shoulders and I fall back on yard stones. The
foal stands over me and his lips tickle my face and
wriggle into my hair. My wrist is sprained. My mother
and Joe come running and slap the foal and shout . . . Get
off . . . go on . . . get away . . . and the foal's head goes up
and his ears lie back and his eyes roll.

I shout . . . Don't . . . don't . . . he's frightened . . . he
doesn't understand. I get up crying and put my arms

round his neck and twist his new black wiry mane in my fingers.

My mother says . . . It is high time he learns he is a pony and not a person.

One evening coming home from Granny's I fall asleep in the car until my mother says . . . Wake up . . . out you get . . . run indoors . . . I can't hear the electric . . . it must have stopped . . . I've got to go and look. The night is pitch black. The coal shed oak has disappeared. I reach for the kitchen door handle and lean in the doorway and slip in slime and fall on small sharp things that crack and break and prickle. I get on all fours and reach forward and touch a sideboard knob and hold on and pull up and my slimy hand slips off and I slither and fall again. I hear footsteps over by the Esse cooker and roll sideways in the mess and sit up and listen . . . one two three four . . . one two . . . the foal is walking towards me on flagstones.

My mother comes to the door and shines torchlight in my eyes and round the kitchen. The foal is neighing a high murmur and my mother is laughing. She leans against the doorpost and points the torchlight. The white tin egg bowl is upside down on the ground. Raw eggs and broken shells are spread over the flagstones. I say . . . What's happened . . . it's disgusting . . . and my mother says . . . Mister Foal started making scrambled eggs for us . . . he's opened the kitchen door all by himself.

She shines the torch on the foal and says . . . You got in the kitchen on your own . . . didn't you . . . yes you think you are a very clever boy . . . don't you? She shines torchlight on me and giggles and says . . . Raw egg's s'posed to be good for the complexion . . .

I say . . . I'm going to be sick . . .

She says . . . Up you get . . . hold onto the sideboard . . . take off your coat and shoes and socks . . . get a drying-up cloth and wipe as much off as you can. I've got to go back out and get the electric restarted. You take a candle and run a bath straight away. The water will only be luke-warm . . . unless the engine kept running till not long ago. Rinse your hair in the basin and wrap a towel round it and get into bed . . . you will have to sleep with it wet . . . it can't be helped. Come on foaly . . . you come out with me to the engine shed . . . if we're lucky there will be light and I will be able to see to clean up this cookery mess you've made . . . come along . . . follow me.

I pick eggshell chips off my face and smear them on my blue tweed coat and do what my mother says. I pull the bathroom light cord and suddenly light comes on.

By autumn the foal is weaned off milk onto bread and carrots and lawn mowings and starts to graze. My mother leads a Welsh pony and Hug-Me-Tight down the lane to the Valley. The other Welshies and Hug-Me's foal follow and I walk behind with Kiss-Me's foal. When cold weather comes we ride over and herd the ponies up to Needlehole and the Windmill thorn thickets to shelter from wind and snow.

At two years I ride the foal. I sit on his back and he turns his head and goes in circles and nuzzles my toes. My mother says . . . We'll have to find someone else for the job . . . he will never be worth a penny. He cannot forget it is you. The gypsies could put him in shafts and get him going straight that way . . . they will be at Stow Fair next month.

No . . . I shout . . . The gypsies can't have him . . . I'll never see him again ever . . . that's so cruel . . . it's unfair . . . Kiss-Me-Quick's happy in her lovely new home . . . and he's never been mean to anyone . . . not once . . . ever in his whole life.

My mother says . . . Perhaps the Gartrells would have him . . . they want a pony just to play with . . . I'll write to Joy tonight.

My mother drives Merrylegs in the green and yellow Ralli-cart to Andoversford station and I sit facing backwards and lead the foal. He follows me up the train ramp into the dark and I kiss his nose and say . . . I'll come and see you. I wave at the train and smoke passes the pines.

My mother says . . . They'll love having him in the commuter belt . . . do you think Merrylegs knows he is her grandson . . . do you Merry . . . do you know that handsome young fellow who caught Kiss-Me-Quick in the branches in Sheep Pen is your son Mervyn . . . now for the post office to telegram Joy time of his arrival.

11

HORSE

On a windy day in springtime daffodils hiss and I break off flowers and stalks squeak. Half a mile away up the drive a gearbox screeches as the jeep turns in the red iron gate. The engine revs before Sheep Dip hump and wheel springs thud and link chains rattle and tyres bump in and out of potholes and couplings rub and I see our blue two-wheeler horse trailer sway wildly side to side down the yard. I run across the lawn and put my daffodils on the garden wall.

My father says . . . Stand back . . . here comes a big surprise. He pulls out tailgate ratchets and opens the ramp. A thin fleabitten grey racehorse clatters down ridged coconut matting and stops dead still. His black eyes stare above our heads up Homefield. His eyelashes are white.

The corners of his lips are cut. Scab patches blacken his saddle patch and withers and girth.

I step forward to stroke the horse's face. His backside swerves at me and his narrow hooves scatter yard stones. I see his tail dock is rubbed to bristle. He kicks out a hind leg and swings his face my way and shows his black-eyed teeth. My father says ... Keep back ... I told you ... bloody child ... unless you want to get yourself killed ... stand back I say.

I catch the knotted end of the head-collar rope swinging past and move my hands up the cord. My mother comes behind me and says ... Let him loose. The horse breathes fast treading backwards and watches us.

My father says ... Steady on old boy ... nicely does it ... you've had one hell of a time ... any damned fool can see that ... you'll be right as rain from now on ... the word of a cavalry officer old man ... we'll have you back in top-notch form in no time ... yes my friend ... you're safely home now ... no more bad times for you ... can you reach the rope to knot it up Bear ... go gently now ... tie the end up off the ground ... good boy ... stand where you are ... no one's going to hurt you ... that's nicely done ... now all move back ... gently does it ... I vote we leave him to meet the poultry ... run up and close the top yard gate child ... get a move on . . . before he heads for the main road . . . or else we'll see all hell break loose.

I run up and back and my father says . . . A six-year-old by Persian Gulf out of a mare by Royal Minstrel . . . can you beat it . . . so-and-sos at some second-rate racing stable let him get into this disgraceful condition. People like that ought to be shot in my opinion. This horse was bred to win the Derby. It's the same old story . . . unsuccessful blood horse kept and used as a pacemaker . . . no bets for stable boys on him so . . . who cares. Racing is all for worshippers of Mammon these days . . . like every other damn thing.

My mother says . . . Where did you find him . . . and my father says . . . I set out secretly for Newmarket this morning. On the off chance I'd find a nice mare cheap at Mr Tattersall's spring sale to bring you girls as an Easter egg. Saw him in the ring going for a song. He'll be a star when he makes himself at home . . . won't that be something to show off about . . . yes old boy . . . take all the time you want . . . quietly set about making yourself welcome.

I give my mother the daffodils and climb onto the apple tree scabby fork and watch the racehorse through the apple blossom. He arches his long neck down and herds the flock of Chinese geese up the yard and blows his nostrils to wide dark rings. The geese turn and face him and walk backwards on webbed feet and bulbous heels and bow snake bows and hiss.

The grey horse snorts and trots. The geese fan out and honk half-flying-half-running and their wingtips reach high as the horse's belly. The racehorse trots at a cockerel and hens and veers off to Homefield gate and scents the mares up by Fishpond Wood. He stamps and neighs.

The mares' heads lift and they start downhill at a walk ... and a trot ... and gallop and stiffen front legs on gateway ruts and slide to a stop and hang heads over the gate top bar. The racehorse breathes on each mare's face.

Indoors my father says ... Any news to report ... one slice of hot buttered toast reserved for you. I have permitted myself a celebration ... extra lashings of Mr Fortnum's and Mr Mason's Gentleman's Relish ... known by intellectual types with a classical education as Patum Peperium. Followed by a monster slice of your mother's snipe-bog cake ... strictly forbidden to colonels weighing over fourteen stone ... hey-ho.

My mother says ... I'm short of duck eggs ... one duck is sitting in Calfpen nettles ... it is such a pity ... she'll get eaten one of these nights.

My father says ... Shoot the bloody fox if you want my advice ... my money is on the old dog fox Gaussen harbours in his cover ... a fox that keeps a pack of

hounds running for eight miles will soon discover a decent meal sitting there a field away from his earth. You might consider tying a string to your duck's leg at night and knot the other end to a tin bucket . . . under a clear night sky there's a sporting chance I'll get a successful pot-shot from our bedroom window when the bucket rattles and Gaussen's fox runs for home.

He opens Homefield gate and the thin grey horse flares nostrils and blows over the mares' backs as they pass. My mother leans across the gate and unclips his head rope and says . . . You are your own master now . . . so you be good.

The racehorse sets out at a gallop in the Valley and my father says . . . Take a damned good look at that, everybody . . . Christ what a mover . . . you won't see a show like that every day of the week . . . in a class of his own.

He'll fatten up like butter on spring grass and we'll fetch him in in June. He'll eat out of my hand by July . . . God willing. If Prime Minister Eden hasn't sent us – quite wrongly in my opinion – to war over Suez he'll carry my Bear hunting by Christmas. You will look the cat's whiskers . . . make no mistake. What a day that will be . . . to see a horse like that enjoy himself . . . yes siree . . . enough coffee-housing . . . I shall soak my body in a bath of spanking hot water fragrantly scented with Mr Boot's finest pine essence and lie back and contemplate the foolishness of those in power and the pleasure of seeing a lovely horse gallop down a valley. He sings . . . Vilja, oh Vilja, for ever be true . . .

I slosh pine essence into his running bath and he says . . . Steady on now . . . steady on . . . moderation in all things . . . isn't that what the Almighty preaches . . . *è pericoloso sporgese* . . . which correctly translated from the Italian means it is dangerous to lean out of the window. Remember that. A foreign phrase can prove useful in a tight corner . . . off you go.

In June the grey horse comes up the lane with the mares. He is fat as a barrel and good as gold. Then he nearly kills my father in the stable and my mother says to me . . . Do as I say . . . don't go near . . . he has bad memories to fight . . . he will calm down . . . given time.

My father makes detours past the stable. The horse

huddles in a far corner and strikes a hind hoof at white-washed brick walls. My father lobs in apple slices and carrots and lumps of sugar. A week later the horse takes a step or two forward if my father approaches and after a fortnight he snatches food off my father's open hand. In July his head hangs over the stable door and he blows warm breath over my father's face and hands.

At harvest time I gallop a pony across rattling stubble and see my father leading the horse along woodland paths. The horse learns to stand quietly by a tractor while my father strips ears of corn with a finger and thumb, and bites on grains to test for ripeness and sieves corn through his fingers for thistle seeds and wild oats and makes harvest plans with Joe Rummings.

I ride behind the horse in gulley lanes past mauve foxgloves and purple loosestrife and white blackberry flowers and hear my father say . . . Mind out where you go old boy . . . no knocking the colonel over . . . it seems the Almighty thinks we deserve a little something special . . . He has certainly sent us a perfect summer's day if ever I saw one . . . now where is that bloody dog . . . here . . . good dog . . . come to master . . . heel . . . I say heel. That's more like it . . . time to brush up your manners . . . take a lesson from my friend here. Isn't that right old boy . . . no going to exciting places if we can't behave. Good dog . . . off you go . . . good dog . . . rabbits . . . seek . . . seek 'em out. The spaniel zigzag tracks up grass banks. Her speckled nose sniffs the ground. Her black stub tail wags. In the standing corn she leaps up and her black ears flap and disappear in barley gold.

In autumn my father rides the grey horse. One morning he canters across Airplane Field and the girth is loose. The saddle slips and he is pulled under the horse's belly and his foot twists and catches in a stirrup iron. The horse drags my father at a canter on stony ground in sharp wheat stubble and slows to a trot and a walk and stands still. My father lies on his back by the horse's hind hooves and says . . . Thank you old boy . . . that is a great deal more than I could reasonably expect of you . . . stay as you are . . . we'll see if the Almighty can come up with a solution to our predicament.

Joe Rummings is driving a tractor and four-furrow

plough and turning at the far end of Airplane Field. The
tractor engine stops and my father hears Joe's footsteps
in the ground coming nearer. He says to the horse . . .
Now old boy . . . listen to what I say . . . there seems to be
a chance in a million this shemozzle can be resolved . . .
wouldn't that be something . . . so you listen carefully . . .
old Joe is coming across . . . he will take a few minutes
. . . Airplane is a damned big field by Cotswold standards . . . nothing of course to the acreages the East
Anglian johnnies cultivate . . . up there a plough runs in a
straight line across a hundred acres. What we have to
keep in mind is that old Joe is damned windy about
horses. That's the most important fact I want you to
remember . . . and don't forget either that Joe could
perfectly easily have kept on ploughing . . . yes sir. The
colonel learned a thing or two in wartime old boy. It is
frequently not the enemy. It is what fear does that gets
you killed. I have requested extra help from those above
who I trust are watching . . . *è pericoloso sporgese* . . . here
we go . . .

. . . Hello Joe . . . thank you for coming over . . . will
you do exactly as I say. Walk round this side and take the
old boy's rein in your left hand. First rate . . . take hold of
both girth buckle straps in your right hand. When I tell
you pull down damned hard. With luck the buckles will
release. That done you let go smartly. When the saddle

falls on the floor the old boy will most probably make off. Let him go. That won't matter a damn. I'll catch him later. Have you got that clear? Right . . . no time like the present.

The saddle hits the stubble and the horse dances sideways and snorts and my father tugs the stirrup iron off his foot. He stands up and takes the horse's rein from Joe. He strokes the long arched grey neck and pulls from his pocket a half apple and a white sugar lump. The horse nuzzles my father's sweater and wriggles his top lip white hairstar in my father's palm and my father says . . . That's my boy . . . what a fellow you are . . . a proper star . . . thank you Joe. It was good of you to walk all the way over. Haven't let a saddle slip since I played polo against the Argentinians at Roehampton in 1936. On that occasion I was damned lucky to stay alive. Perhaps the Almighty has something else in mind to keep me occupied. I had thought surviving wartime was all I could reasonably ask of Him and from then on I'd face the consequences of my mistakes. Hey-ho . . . good to see the ploughing is progressing. Wireless says a bloody east wind is due. Return home immediately that occurs. It can get cold as hell up here . . . as you well know. I'll walk the old boy over by the wall. Too old to climb aboard any more without a stepping stone. Thank you again Joe.

After that day my father says I can ride the grey racehorse. He watches us trot up the yard and says . . . You two look a million dollars . . . what did I tell you. You could do a lot worse than listen to an old colonel. Mark my words. The pair of you will be the envy of the Cotswold field. I would not be at all surprised if you bring home a One Day Event silver pot . . . if you both practise dressage and showjumping. He will do the cross-country on his head . . . you will only need to sit tight and point him in the right direction.

Before a day's hunting I stretch rubber over-reach boots over the horse's front feet to protect his pastern heels. One day we jump a wall into wet clay plough and a field later a man leans off his horse beside me and says . . . I say . . . you've put your horse's boot on a back foot . . .

won't perform any useful function there . . . off in cloud cuckoo land when you saddled up . . . were you? I say . . . he must have changed his boots round by himself.

I write to *The Field* . . . Have any readers experience of an over-reach boot changed from front to back hoof by a horse? Letters reply . . . Suggest the suction effect of clay . . . once saw a horse pick up his saddle in his teeth and throw it on his own back. My mother says . . . He is rather famous now . . . people stop me out hunting and ask to see him change his boots.

My father says . . . Damned silly . . . the hoi polloi . . .

The autumn I leave home my father says . . . The old boy's getting on . . . one more season at most I'd say . . . don't want to see him lose condition.

I come back at weekends to go hunting on him. One cold Saturday in March I drive the horse trailer to Compton Abdale. My Hunting Diary says . . . Very cold . . . found in Lawrence's Gorse . . . ran via Shipton Oliffe to ground at Hasleton . . . five miles.

At the end of the day at the trailer my cold fingers fumble throatlash buckle and curb-chain hooks and the head collar. I lead the horse to the ramp and say . . . Come on lovely boy . . . home we go. The tall grey racehorse rears sideways and his back legs jump slanted pulley wire and his front hoof strikes ramp matting. He bites my dark-blue hunting jacket sleeve and I say . . . Be

careful . . . mind the wire . . . go back . . . that's it . . .
gently . . . now let's start again. I rub his forehead and
hold a ginger biscuit on the palm of my hand and the
horse dances and rears and his hooves clatter on tarmac.
I say . . . Come on my boy . . . it is cold . . . get in . . . time
to go home.

He stands on the road and I slap his shoulder with
the rope end and shout . . . Get on
. . . get up there . . . ruddy horse.
I stroke his face and scratch his
forelock and whisper . . .
Sweetheart . . . what is it . . .
it's all alright . . . I love you
. . . yes I do . . . my boy.

I sit on the ramp and say
. . . Go ahead . . . stand there all
night . . . why don't you want to go home . . . tell me . . .
we'll freeze to death together on this hill. The horse
looks over my head at brown and green fields rolling
away to St Paul's Epistle where the farm begins.

Under the jeep front seat is a bottle of cherry brandy in
a brown paper bag. My father says . . . You never can
anticipate when damned machinery will break down and
you will be caught out in bloody awful weather . . . a
tincture keeps body and soul together . . . you mark
my words.

I tip the bottle to my lips and sickly alcohol burns my throat. I pour a splash on a handful of hay and the horse nibbles and flaps his long tongue and wrinkles his lips and his brown teeth grin. I drink from the bottle and sit on the ramp. The horse shivers and winter dark begins. The grey horse walks suddenly past me and noses my head and goes in the trailer. I stand up and raise the tailboard and slam in ratchets and set off for home.

I overtake a lorry at Frogmill turn. The trailer sways and hooves clatter. I swing in the red gate and scrape the post. In the yard I steer to the barn and park against the hay bale rick and run indoors. My father comes out and opens the ramp and says to the horse . . . What have you two been up to old boy . . . you both look considerably the worse for wear.

I lie on my bed and the ceiling whirls and my mother says . . . Drink this . . . it will make you sick . . . hurry up . . . do as I say . . . drink it all . . . it is not right to treat a lovely horse like that . . . you should be ashamed of yourself . . . he might have been badly hurt . . . the roads are dangerous enough as it is . . . alcohol and driving do not mix.

One summer day I lead the grey horse up to Rickyard between the muck heap and Sheep Pen larches near a Cotswold Hunt covered trailer with a chain and pulley inside the open ramp. I rub his grey face and give him sugar lumps and apple slices on my palm and say to a kennel huntsman in a brown overall with a stun-gun in his hand . . . All right . . . you can do it now. I stroke the arched grey neck and tickle his top lip star. The gun goes up between the horse's big dark eyes and the man's first finger moves and the grey racehorse is dead. His head lowers and he stumbles and falls over sideways on hard rickyard ground and daisies and dandelions and dirty brown straw. I walk down the yard and lean on his stable and watch Chinese geese sitting close together in sunshine and the hens and black creosoted doors on stables and barns and the yard stones.

My mother comes out and says . . . Drive down to church with me and we'll do the flowers . . . there will be people there from Withington and Chedworth who will remember you . . . they're there flattening out graves to make the churchyard easier to mow.

I say . . . Where is Big Bear . . . and my mother says . . . He'll be at the church too . . . come on . . . you can say your prayers and light a candle . . . then you will feel a lot better.

12

CHRISTMAS

The first Christmas after wartime my father plays the *Merry Widow* waltz on the radiogram and dances my mother round the oval dining-room table and reverse waltzes on the Persian rug between the table and the spinette sideboard in his chalk-striped grey flannel suit and cream silk shirt and brown brogues. He says . . . Now we'll have some fun . . . and sings . . . Vilja, oh Vilja, for ever be true . . .

My mother wears an apron over her tweed skirt and knitted green jersey and pearl necklace and says . . . I hope I've made enough mince pies for everyone . . . I'm surprised at Great-Aunt Alice and Granny falling fast asleep by the drawing-room fire for so long.

My father says . . . I'll be a good boy and confess . . . I

deposited a thermos of Cognac and hot water in Granny's Austin Devon . . . reasoning if old Alice's train arrives late at the station she'll take a nip and suffer less from the cold. Plus . . . I anticipated the two old girls driving straight past our red gate on their way home and realising their mistake at Seven Springs crossroads. A soupçon of hot brandy builds up courage like nobody's business and the bends on the steep hill back up Chatcombe are slippery as hell.

My mother says . . . I saw them through the window jiggy as leprechauns. I do hope *le* Voss family will find their way here . . . we are a very long drive from the east coast Harwich car ferry.

My father sits down on a mahogany dining-room chair and says . . . I shall never forget my first encounter with Jules Voss. It was eight months after the Normandy landing. I stood on the side of a lane in the Ardennes Forest in the dark and a voice from on horseback asked in

deplorable English if I would like a hot bath and to sleep the night in a bed with clean sheets. God knows how Jules reached the regiment unharmed under the noses of the Boche. Plus he had no earthly reason to leave the safety of his own home. Decent Belgiques endured one hell of a war. People tend to forget. And by the same token we must not forget the Dutch. Uncle Willy and Aunt Misha will arrive in style on Christmas Eve at the start of festivities.

My mother says ... I only wish Alec were here as well ... thank heavens his Atlantic convoy days are a thing of the past.

The day before Christmas Eve Jules Voss in spec-tacles and jodhpurs and a tweed jacket and trilby runs up the yard swinging a short-handled wood chopper round his head. Chinese geese turn on him and hiss and flap. Jules lets the handle go. The chopper flies. The tallest gander

walks backwards headless. My mother says . . . Oh dear . . . that's the grandfather . . . I am afraid he may be quite tough.

Granny says . . . That is a nice quick way to kill a goose.

The two Voss children jump up and down and call out . . . Papa . . . Papa.

Great-Aunt Alice holds a black tin trumpet to her ear and shouts . . . Is that man off his head . . . who is he.

My father shouts into the trumpet . . . A damned good Christmas feast coming our way Alice. The headless gander sits on yard stones and blood runs from his neck.

Jules Voss says . . . *C'est tout à fait bien . . . oui.*

My mother says . . . It's very good Jules . . . *très bien . . . merci beaucoup.* The black-and-white spaniel picks up the gander's head and trots to Homefield gate and wriggles under and disappears behind the stables.

In the kitchen my mother and Jules's wife Christiane pluck the gander and shove goose down inside a white cotton pillowcase and speak French. At the dining-room table Granny and Great-Aunt Alice silently wipe dust off china with linen cloths. Crown Derby pudding plates in gold and black and orange. Creamy rippling Copenhagen china.

The goose goes in the Esse oven and my mother lights paraffin lamps and spreads brown paper on the dining-room table and lays out silver forks and spoons and silver

pheasants and challenge cups and the silver tray. The
two Voss children and I and Christiane polish silver with
torn-up strips of summer dresses and hand-knitted jersey
squares.

My father and Jules come in carrying guns and dead
pheasants and my father says . . . First class the troops . . .
keep it up . . . Jules and I will set about concocting a rum
punch to knock your whiskers off.

Great-Aunt Alice says loudly . . . What is he saying . . .
for the Lord God Almighty's sake will no one write
words down.

Before the 11 a.m. Cotswold Hounds Christmas Eve
meet up at Gaussen's I polish my father's black top hat
with a crimson spotted silk handkerchief. He rides up
the drive on Golden Glory beside my mother riding the
Lion of Judah's half-sister Princess Victoria. Jules Voss
rides Merrylegs the Ralli-cart bay dock-tailed Welsh cob.
Griff leads me on my black pony Darkie. My father's pink
coat-tails hang over Golden Glory's saddle. My mother's
young chestnut mare's four white-stocking legs dance.
Jules Voss pulls up his stirrup leathers jockey short. Griff
takes a green-and-gold lidded tin from his pocket and a
bone-handled penknife and slices a tobacco cake and
says to me . . . You'll like my sweet baccy. I put a lump on
my tongue and suck and spit and Griff chews his.

In Gaussen's field hounds jump at Christiane and the

Voss children. A whipper-
in cracks a white whiplash
and growls . . . Down,
Mercy . . . Lady . . . git-on-
back.

My mother leans off
her chestnut mare and
holds a little glass out to
me and says . . . Try a sip of port . . . it's very warming.
I swallow and screw up my face. A man in a black jacket
and striped trousers offers me a slice of plum cake on a
silver salver. Granny and Great-Aunt Alice stand by
Gaussen's garden gate in long dark-blue skirts and fur
coats and black felt hats pinned with pheasant and
partridge feathers.

Master in a scarlet coat and green collar and white
breeches blows a note on his copper horn and stands up
in his stirrups and says . . . Good to see you all . . . some
faces missing . . . we ride out today in memory of their
bravery . . . a happy Christmas to you all . . . h'up, little
ladies . . . good girls . . . good little bitches . . . y'ew'on.
He rides down Gaussen's track towards the farm and
hounds run into Fishpond Wood.

Wild duck fly out of treetops quacking and my midnight-blue velvet hunting cap cork lining presses on my
forehead and I say to Griff . . . Can we go home.

Twisted red candles in tin spring-snap holders bend down Christmas tree branches. Red ribbon bows are tied on the tree and silver tinsel shivers. A gold painted cardboard star touches the drawing-room ceiling. Under the tree brown paper parcels and red and green crêpe paper packages are tied with string. Firelight shines in the brass rings around the mahogany Irish peat bucket the tree stands in.

By teatime on Christmas Eve punch is hot in a copper urn on the Esse. My mother comes in from milking and says ... Somebody count chairs ... I make us sixteen in all ... leaving out children. I'll fill up paraffin stoves and then dress. Jules ... will you keep up the fire ... *s'il vous plaît*.

Jules says ... *Ma chérie* ... I am *entièrement pour toi* ... and Christiane says ... *Alors* ... *tu as la bonne chance*.

Granny says ... Shall I wear Mr Silver Fox-Fur or Mr Black ... and Great-Aunt Alice says ... I cannot hear you, Eva ... I have told you before ... you speak far too softly ... make yourself clear ... or for the Lord's sake write down what you wish to say to me.

My father says ... A god-awful noise I recognise is approaching.

An accordian wheezes outside the drawing-room window and Mrs Fish sings ... Once in royal David's city ...

My father takes a goose sandwich off a plate and

bites and says ... Dear God ... the damned goose is inedible ... tough as leather ... I damned near broke my new false teeth ... we can't have this ... jump to it, everyone. Return all sandwiches to kitchen headquarters. We'll roast our Christmas Day lunch pheasants double quick. Jules to carve. Christiane, remove all goose and replace with pheasant. I'll keep the old boys drinking as long as is necessary. I don't want the Griffs and Joe and Mundays treated like servants ... do I make myself clear. An hour should just about do it. My Bear won't be entirely happy ... needs must when the devil drives. Hey-ho ... scrambled eggs on the menu for Christmas lunch tomorrow. He throws goose slices to the spaniel and puts on his white bearskin coat and turns up the black fur collar and opens the kitchen door.

Mrs Fish stops singing. Her shiny turquoise and chrome accordion curves open and sighs. She sways and winks at my father and stands up on tiptoe in red muddy high-heeled leather boots and whispers ... Betty's Christmas box ready Colonel?

My father says ... If you will forgive me ... I am off to give a special Christmas treat to the beloved horses ... before I line up the rest of the troops. He looks back at us and says ... No disobeying orders.

General Wilhelm Roëll arrives in a chauffeur-driven car. My father says ... *mon Général* ... my dear Aunt

Misha . . . let me introduce . . . my wife . . . my small daughter . . . *et le Capitaine Jules Voss* . . . premier race-horse trainer *dans la Belgique* . . . Mr and Mrs Griffin of Kilkenny . . . my mother-in-law Eva . . . her sister Miss Alice Lenox-Conyngham from Ulster . . . Joe Rummings from Foxcote . . . Mrs Fish and daughter Betty from Needlehole . . . *les* Voss children *et leur mère Christiane* . . . and Mr and Mrs Munday from Keeper's Cottage. A great honour, *mon Général* . . . a glass of hot punch for Uncle Willy please . . . and a glass of lemonade for Aunt Misha . . . will your driver join the party?

My father and mother stand in front of the fireplace in the drawing room and he says . . . A toast to my uncle . . . General Wilhelm Roell . . . who showed immense cour-age under conditions of severe deprivation. Captured early on during the invasion of Holland and kept prisoner in a cellar ... water ankle-deep below his bunk. An ordeal lasting for three hellish years. A spirit of courage I have frequently encountered among the Dutch.

Aunt Misha holds a black-and-yellow round sweet tin and Uncle Willy says ... To the joyous memory of the Hopje ... a bon-bon created by Rademaker our famous Dutch sweetmaker for my own and the colonel's ancestor ... a past prime minister of Holland incapacitated by caffeine ... as am I ... and *mon colonel*. Aunt Misha opens the tin and hands round small square toffees. Uncle Willy pulls a little red-and-gold leather-bound book from his pocket and gives it to me and says ... English poetry ... excellent with Hopjes ... you will one day discover.

My father and Jules take round jugs of punch and fill Irish Waterford cut-glass tumblers. Christiane and my mother offer plates of pheasant sandwiches and Mrs Griff cuts the iced Christmas cake  decorated with silver- and gold-painted fir cones, a Father Christmas and a china church. My father raises his glass and says ... A toast to Alec ... my absent naval officer brother ... the socialist in our family.

My mother says ... I would like to say a thank you to

everyone here this Christmas who has worked on the farm these wartime years.

Mrs Fish's accordion plays 'Hark the Herald Angels'. We all sing. My father's tenor voice takes the high descant

parts. Granny writes on Great-Aunt Alice's writing pad that hangs off her waist, 'Hark the Herald' and 'While Shepherds Watched' and 'In the Bleak'.

My mother lifts me up and says . . . Christmas Day tomorrow . . . off you go to sleep . . . if Father Christmas finds you awake remember you'll get lumps of coal in your stocking.

I cry and my father says . . . What's this . . . a colonel's daughter bellyaching on Christmas Eve . . . what say we light the Christmas tree candles. Stand by for a first-class conflagration of velvet curtains. He claps his hands and says . . . Christmas tree lighting will in theory be followed by presents . . . followed by a secret I have all prepared . . . Charlie Chaplin on screen no less. Next Christmas . . . God willing . . . I shall show cinefilm shot on the farm in the year ahead. Take your places on all available chairs. Thank you, Mrs Fish. Now a Strauss waltz on the radiogram . . . before the show begins . . .

who shall I put in command. Volunteers please . . . those not yet well on the road to getting nicely foxed . . . and he looks my way and puts his finger to his lips and winks.

My mother says . . . As it's Christmas you can stay up with Betty and *les* Voss children. We are all safely here at last . . . now I shall light the tree candles . . . if I'm lucky . . . you gallop on.

13

GALLOP AWAY

In summer 1953 Elizabeth II is crowned Queen and I go away from home to a girls' school in a castle. In London my mother and I watch the coronation parade pass along Piccadilly from upstairs in the Cavalry Club. My father is Deputy Crown Equerry and stands at the door of Westminster Abbey to step forward and welcome foreign royalty arriving in horse-drawn carriages.

After the coronation he leaves the army and comes home to the farm. He spends my mother's money like water. Farm machinery ... modern fertilisers ... pedigree Hereford beef cattle ... high class port. In school holidays I gallop after him round the farm jumping fences and he yells ... Legs ... use your bloody legs.

My mother says to me years later . . . I did wonder where my daughter had gone.

Their tragedy gets going hell for leather. She is in the kitchen and in her bedroom more every day. He shouts at night in his room. He rushes to the bathroom through my bedroom in a tartan flannel dressing gown. He lies on my blue eiderdown and hugs me tightly and says . . . Snuggly buggly Little Bear . . . snuggly snuggly buggly.

My mother tiptoes in and he stands up fast and bends and tugs my eiderdown straight and says . . . I was discussing tying the Lion of Judah's head down tight in a standing martingale to teach him a proper lesson . . . hey-ho . . . off into the arms of Morpheus . . . good night, Bears . . . may God bless you . . . and he sings . . . The Lord is my shepherd, I shall not want . . . along the back passage to his room.

My mother smooths the eiderdown and says . . . A loose-running martingale is all the Lion needs.

It rains and I tidy up my father's sock drawer. Woolly

socks to the back. Silk to the front. Cotton in between. By his chest of drawers mirror is a framed photograph of a girl smiling. I don't know her. She's not my mother. In a second photograph a different girl in a pleated skirt and curvy jacket stands by a signpost 'Rotterdam 32km . . . Leiden 12km' and this girl smiles in another silver frame. There is a black framed photograph of my Uncle Alec in naval uniform. No photos of my mother or me.

A small snap of Bozo a curly-haired Airedale dog is stuck in his mirror corner. In wartime Bozo chases a

rabbit past a tractor my father is turning in the field pulling a haycutter and cutter knives slice off the dog's four legs. My mother has her 16 bore gun with her in the hayfield and shoots the dog. She writes in her diary . . . Those knives in the hayfield . . . oh Bozo.

On Sundays for church my father wears a handmade grey pinstripe suit with a dark-green spotted silk handkerchief in his breast pocket. He leaves for church early and flirts with choirgirls. All his life he trains choirs with a passion for the music. He sings tenor at Dowdeswell church and directs the singing from the choir stalls looking over bifocal gold-rimmed spectacles.

My mother puts on a racing-green velvet beret hat and a tweed coat and drives up to church as the service begins. She kneels in a back pew and whispers prayers . . . Forgive us our trespasses as we forgive those who trespass against us . . .

The service ends and she drives off. He loiters in church and coffee houses with the choristers and the con-gregation and argues with the vicar . . . The Sermon on the Mount is . . . you will no doubt agree . . . the only . . . I repeat only . . . verifiable words of our Lord . . . and should by any standards be included in Matins.

At home she takes Sunday lunch out of the oven and carries it through to the dining room and eats alone. Or with me. She leaves his lunch on the sideboard to get cold. Roast chicken and fresh vegetables and bread sauce and gravy. He comes home and says . . . Damned chicken is the temperature of a tepid bath. She is upstairs in her room.

In school holidays I drive to church with my mother or father on alternate Sundays each and I pray . . . Dear Jesus . . . what will happen?

I am at college when my mother cracks her skull in

her hunting accident. I come home again to look after the house and horses and my father. I ride and cook and speak to her friends and learn typing and Pitman's Shorthand in Cheltenham. I say to him . . . Try not to bang all the doors . . . it makes her headache worse.

While she is away in hospital I tidy her room. Under her brown mesh stockings is a steamed open blue envelope addressed to him in a handwriting I've never seen.

My darling Bumble, You are a very patient Bumbly teacher. I am a very happy girl. Can hardly wait three more days. All my love from your impatient Bumbly.

I pair up stockings. Silk and nylon in front. Criss-cross mesh between. Wool at the back. I throw away the letter and say to her . . . I threw away a letter in your stocking drawer.

Her eyes fill with tears and she says . . . I do wish you'd leave my things alone.

They arrive together for my girls' boarding school Saturday night dance. He says to me . . . Now we'll show them all a thing or two . . . and waltzes and reverse waltzes me to 'The Blue Danube' in between a hundred girls while she sits at the side of the room on a Pell chair beside the deaf headmistress.

She writes to me when I am working in MI5 offices in London.

> . . . I am so sorry, darling . . . I am afraid I do not make
> Daddy happy . . . the Irish furniture that will be yours one
> day is moving to the rectory in Whittington . . . I shall
> have four rooms there all of my own . . . my drawing room
> faces south . . . I shall enjoy the sun shining in.

I open her letter after bicycling home to a flat after work and I hug the blue writing paper with the engraved address – Pegglesworth, Andoversford, nr Cheltenham, Glos. Tel. Andoversford 267. I stare out at the street and see again exactly how the farmyard sparkles on a winter morning and fox prints mark white frost and icicles shine over stable doors and the horses' breath is clouds and she looks into a stable over a half-door and says to her chest-nut mare . . . Very glamorous white whiskers . . . out you come . . . have a play in the lovely white yard . . . go on . . . roll over . . . paw paw . . . careful you don't slip . . . and she says to me . . . Look up at the granary . . . foxy is always gold in a sky this blue . . . see the water trough . . . green ice . . . and the hens are doing a high-step-wait-step . . . quite elegant . . . Edwardian . . . such a beautiful day so far.

And I remember 'Dancing Cheek to Cheek' playing on

the radiogram and him saying . . . High time I take a turn
with my Bear . . . and I follow him into the dining room
and sit on a chair and he foxtrots her round the oval
mahogany table. My legs stick out and he says . . . Move
out of the way child.

He stays on at the farm after she leaves and breeds
Hereford beef cattle and shouts at herdsmen and writes
to me

> . . . a top-rate new chap arrives next week . . . a higher
> calibre altogether from the last disaster I had to get rid of
> in a hurry. Three young bulls coming on are the cat's
> whiskers and will put us out of the red in the farm account
> I am certain.

After my mother has left I go home and girls from
Cheltenham I don't know are grooming the horses and
he says . . . Everyone into the jeep . . . jump to it all of
you . . . time for a jolly.

We drive round the farm hell for leather and the girls
scream . . . Stop . . . stop Colonel . . .

He says . . . The elder Stottie daughter at the rectory
has achieved her final exams and I am paying for her to
have her bedroom redecorated as a congratulation. He
takes a farmer's fair-haired daughter to London to lunch
in the Cavalry Club and says . . . Good for her to know

how the other half behave in town. He writes, 'The *church choir go from strength to strength ... we sing at seven hospitals and nursing homes ... rather good I'd say.'*

My mother writes

> *... have been out to dinner with friends three times this*
> *week and have people coming here. Am asked to instruct*
> *at Pony Club Camp and to run local Girl Guides. Riding*
> *for Disabled is well under way. Shall be glad when you*
> *come down and give a hand leading the riders round at*
> *Oriel School. Uncle Alec and Aunt Juliet invite me*
> *out to Malta while Alec is naval Commander-in-Chief*
> *there. Would like to go if the pennies stretch that far.*
> *Am reading the First Lesson in church this Sunday –*
> *Corinthians – I saw through a glass darkly and now I see*
> *face to face. Am very nervous it will go all right.*

A letter arrives for me from him

> ... I am worn out by worrying about the farm overdraft
> and am putting the entire place on the market next month.
> All proceeds to be given to the Church of England. The
> Church Commissioners will, in turn, buy me a house with
> land I can let out for income. I'll install a caravan in a
> field for parsons working in the city slums to holiday in for
> nothing.

He disappears from the farm with his brown-and-white
spaniel dog. No one knows where he is. I consult a

lawyer on how to find him and how my mother's money can be returned to her. He reappears at the farm with the farmer's fair-haired daughter and says ... A heavenly place in Devon is for sale at just the right price to keep me happy until I meet my Maker.

I say ... The farm was bought with the other Bear's money and she farmed all wartime and afterwards up to the coronation.

He says ... I was pretty certain you'd say that ... do as you wish ... I wash my hands of the whole shebang ... I've worked myself to a standstill and I can't go on. I shall enquire as to an Old People's Home in Devon and book myself in.

I sit on the stairs in a house in London with my baby

son in a carrycot and sell the farm on a black dial telephone that has a cord too short to reach to a table. The
farm money is shared between the three of us.

He buys his pretty thatched Devon house with stables
and fields and a garden looking across a small valley and
up to the edge of Dartmoor. He builds a riding school
and a swimming pool and saves horses galore from
the knackers. So many horses eat so much grass he has
no fields to let and not enough income. He cashes in
his colonel's pension and spends the money. His doctor
telephones me and says . . . Your father is suffering from
malnutrition.

I say . . . Did you know he gave this home entirely to
the Church.

The doctor says . . . I didn't . . . I fear he won't get a
penny back out of them . . . they're a mighty tight-fisted
lot . . . I'll do my best to look after him . . . good to talk
to you.

He lives on Mr Bournville's chocolate powder stirred
into milk, and toast with
lashings of Keiler's mar-
malade for breakfast. Heinz
tinned tomato soup at
lunch. He says . . . Tomato's
the boy for me . . . no point
in experimenting with
another kind. His supper is a television dinner from a
garage up his lane. He says . . . Bloody marvellous inven-
tion . . . no washing-up . . . meal comes in silver foil . . .
all tastes like cotton wool mind you. He drinks Ribena
Blackcurrant mixed fifty-fifty with milk before he goes to
bed and no spirits or wine.

Girls come and groom horses and ride and swim. He
says . . . I've never been so happy in all my life. He says
. . . If I only knew how to make ends meet. He says . . .
First-class parson lets me chose my favourite hymns once
a month. He says . . . Every year I am invited to spend
Christmas Day at Powderham Castle . . . the Courtenay
family have lived there for six centuries . . . pretty good
going I'd say.

He says . . . My horses talk to me like children . . .

He dies in the early morning after feeding his horses
in the stables in his slippers and pyjamas and a big wool
jersey, and before going back to bed to read a biography

of his favourite king Louis XIV. He holds a willow pattern cup of Mr Bournville's chocolate powder stirred with milk in his hand.

At his funeral and at his regimental Memorial Service his war-time padre – code name Sunray – takes the Order and we sing . . . Praise my soul the King of heaven . . .

May lives seventeen more years in a house by the Windrush stream six miles from the farm and falls in love with an American professor of music from Yale University who has bonhomie similar to my father at good times and at bad times is as selfish. She has rheumatism and altogether two broken wrists . . . three ribs . . . two collarbones . . . one arm . . . one ankle . . . one knee . . . her skull . . . mostly from riding falls. And arthritis. After she dies I find thirty-two packets of painkillers in her house. You'd never know. She runs her

Cotswold village Guiting Power 'Over Sixties Cherry Club' and another club at Uncle Alec's widow Juliet's farm when she moves there.

She falls on her stairs one day after saying ... That cheese-wire pain in my head has come back ... what do you think it is? She lives for five days in a deepening coma.

I chant ... Lighten our darkness, oh Lord, and by Thy great mercy protect us from the dangers of this night ... I say to her ... Remember our ponies ... Darkie ... Roany-Pony ... Twinkle ... and Twinkle's son Teddums ... and Merrylegs and her son Mervyn ... and Kiss-Me-Quick and her foal Crispin ... and Hug-Me-Tight and her son Nugget ... and Blarney and Crinkle and Crinkle's son the Lion of Judah, and her daughter Princess Victoria, your lovely chestnut mare with her four white stockings. Remember the horses in the Valley. Glory Boy and Pesky and Marmaduke and Pasha and Paddy and Persian Night. I tell her horse and pony memories in the early mornings and sing her hymns at night, 'Fight the Good Fight' and 'He Who Would Valiant Be' and ... There is a green hill far away, without a city wall, where our dear Lord was crucified, He died to save us all. I sing 'Once in Royal David's City' and ... Vilja, oh Vilja, for ever be true ... and 'Dancing Cheek to Cheek'.

Acknowledgements

Thank you to David Godwin, my literary agent. At HarperCollins, to Arabella Pike, Kate Hyde, Annabel Wright, Julian Humphries, Vera Brice and Carol Anderson for their time and care editing and designing and producing the book. To the Hawthornden Trust and my family and friends, especially to Chiz, Peggy, Susannah, Jen, Di, Robin, Lester and Clarey. And to Charlotte May Hardie, my daughter, who lived with wonderful optimism under the same roof as this book.

P.S.

Ideas,
interviews
& features...

Q and A

with Xandra Bingley

Q. You were born in the Second World War, so has being a war baby had an effect on you?

A. Very much, I am very afraid of war, afraid of the violence and the hurt, and afraid of the consequences that get forgotten when a decision to go to war is taken. Victory is a moment. Poverty and emotional recovery take generations.

Q. What did you want to be when you grew up?

A. At seventeen I wanted to save the world from another war I thought was coming. At fourteen I wanted to be a backing singer to Elvis. At twelve I wanted to ride in the Derby on a grey racehorse disguised as a boy – women were not allowed to ride in flat races. At nine I wanted to drive a crane and swing the arm high in the sky. At six I wanted to be a pony.

Q. When and why did you start writing?

A. I suppose I started making up stories in my head as a child on a farm where what happens next is naturally in your mind all the time ... will that cow go through that gate ... what will happen if not ... who will get hurt ... what can I do to create a good cow-go-through-gate story ...

I think I started writing stories down when my life was confusing. Lots of people do that. W.H. Auden said, 'How can I know what I mean till I see what I say?'

Q. What inspired you to write this book?

A. I don't know for sure, but as I went along it seemed to be a way to honour the people I write about. So although the first three versions were unpublishable, and I kept thinking ... oh well ... I'm not a writer ... I'll stop, the writing kept on wanting to happen, and as I learned more about writing, writing became more fun. Although I've spent thirty years as a publisher, often working with new writers, I found I had to start from the beginning, to learn how to learn about writing myself. It was as if I'd spent years leading pony foals around show rings winning prizes, and then tried riding in the Grand National, galloping a big horse over enormous jumps. Guess what ... I fell off.

Q. Do you miss the way of life the book describes?

A. I miss an English sense of trying to do right. English country life used to be more prejudiced but less selfish, which sounds odd. I don't miss the freezing cold houses or the power of the class system. I like hot water and social equality much more. I do miss the silent fields and steam train whistles and barley sugar and taffeta dresses.

Q. When, or if young people read this book, what will their reactions be?

A. They'll think England was another planet then. But a love story is always a love story, and they'll get that. ▶

3

LIFE
at a Glance

Worked for MI5 in
London, and for Buffalo
University Poetry Library,
The Atlantic Monthly in
Boston, and The Kennedy
Institute of Politics at
Harvard University in
America. Lived in Co.
Kildare, Ireland, and in
London worked at Stitt &
Co., Solicitors, read for the
Bar for six months, joined
The New Review, then
Jonathan Cape Publishers,
and ran a Literary Agency
for fifteen years. Lives by
Primrose Hill in London
and has two children and
a grandson.

Q and A *(continued)*

◄ **Q.** Were children bored before television?

A. Yes, but then what started Henri Matisse painting – he was bored. For a child on a farm, work is play and play is work a lot of the time. And though it's not fun being bored, things are happening, are growing, thoughts, fears, wishes, like stories.

Q. What did it feel like to see your book published?

A. Lovely. I was surprised and happy and honoured.

Q. What motivates you to write?

A. A miracle. If you take a blank piece of paper and make lines of squiggles on it, perhaps someone seeing those squiggles reads them, and laughs or cries or feels fear or hate or love. Isn't that a miracle?

Q. Who influenced you most when you were writing your book?

A. I kept a pile of my top ten books on my table to open or just to touch so the spirit of those books were close and might jump into my own writing, and I played tapes of *Dubliners* by James Joyce, and *Sounds From The Hunting Field*, and Strauss waltzes.

Q. What is your next book?

A. D'you know what someone clever once told me: 'Discretion is the rarest human virtue, not the best but the rarest.' ∎

Top Ten
Favourite Books

1. **Letters from My Windmill**
   Alphonse Daudet

2. **Negotiating With the Dead**
   Margaret Atwood

3. **On The Natural History of Destruction**
   W.G. Sebald

4. **War Music**
   Christopher Logue

5. **An essay on Lightness, in Six Memos for the Next Millennium**
   Italo Calvino

6. **Matisse on Art**
   edited by *Jack D. Flam.*

7. **Lester, Return Of a Legend**
   John Karter

8. **The Road to Xanadu**
   John Livingston Lowes

9. **The Blues Line, A Collection of Blues Lyrics from Leadbelly to Muddy Waters**
   compiled by *Eric Sackheim*

10. **The Beak of the Finch, Evolution in Real Time**
    Jonathan Wiener

How My Memory Works

I HAD TO LEARN ABOUT memory. How to go back to the past and visit the world of the dead. Readers contact me and say 'How do you remember so much . . . all the detail . . . I couldn't remember that much . . . even if you paid me to.'

A lot of time alone in a room has to happen. That's what writing usually is because isolation does things. Once I met a man who had been two years in prison in solitary. He told me he'd recited hours of poetry and prose every day. He said he hadn't ever learned the poetry or prose by heart but when he was desperate, memories of what he'd read came to him.

So it seems that details of the past are ours if we can find them. For that I had guides.

Margaret Atwood is a good guide. In her book *Negotiating With the Dead* she says be careful, the dead expect something, be prepared with a gift, and plan how to return safely. In ancient stories the visitor often does not get back safely, and the dead can strike a tough bargain; look at Persephone, or Gilgamesh.

Sometimes I prepared myself by dressing-up to write in my long silk mauve evening skirt and purple silk top and mauve high-heeled pointy suede shoes. I wake early, a habit from helping milk the cows I guess. I'd walk our golden retriever Samuel Sugarcoat up the hill and come home and change from ordinary clothes. It seemed a way to honour the dead. I was taught as a child that you dress with care for the pleasure of whoever you are going to meet.

And dressing-up let me feel safe in my own world. It sent a message to the dead to say I am only visiting you . . . I am not staying . . . even if you are lonely . . . or have more stories to tell, I'm going home when I choose.

I discovered searching for memories to write is a way to say thank you by sending a memory on a journey in a story. In a book about creativity, *The Gift*, by Lewis Hyde, he says that in some so-called primitive societies gifts are received and often passed on. May, my mother in the book, often used the gift principle. I'd give her a box of chocolates and ask her later if she'd liked the chocs, and she'd say, 'Darling, I gave them to Liza, she works so hard, and she found the time to come and see me, I hope you don't mind.' I hadn't read *The Gift* before she died, so I did mind. Now I've learned better. Today my daughter is giving a silver charm, left to her by May, to her friend. So there is a gift that is on a journey, a way of saying thank you to May for something she has passed on. I hope I am saying thank you to the people whose voices appear in this book by writing my memories.

I also learned that forgetfulness can be a monster that can stop memory happening. Monsters are complicated to overcome. Perseus killed Medusa, the Gorgon monster with a hundred heads who turned everyone who looked at her to stone, by attacking her reflection in his bronze shield. Medusa's blood gave birth to a winged horse, Pegasus, who with one blow of his hoof on Mount Helion, where the gods live, made a spring gush forth – and that's where the muses ▶

How My Memory Works *(continued)*

◄ drink. So Perseus's cleverness and courageous sideways look at his monster let creativity happen.

The past can be heavy and to find a lightness in writing, Italo Calvino is a wonderful guide. In one essay on lightness, Calvino quotes Verlaine on writing: 'Light as a bird, not light as a feather.' There's lots to think about in that. For one thing, that quote led me to try writing with almost no adjectives. For another, if writing grows heavy, self-important, showing-off language, the birds zooming and rising and dipping are visible energy flying, inspiration.

What's going on in the present is easily a big distraction from memory, and a lovely verse about that by Christopher Logue is in my room :

> On days when I intend to work
> I clean my room as if I were
> Expecting an important guest.
> That done, I sit and ask myself:
> What can have kept her?

So thank you to anyone who's read this book and found something in it that they'll pass on. So a story begins. ■

If You Loved This,
You Might Like …

Read on

Cider with Rosie
Laurie Lee
This charming memoir of Laurie Lee's childhood in a remote Cotswold village has sold more than 6 million copies. Set in an idyllic pastoral setting, against the backdrop of the Great War, it describes a world that has mostly vanished.

Memoirs of a Fox-Hunting Man
Siegfried Sassoon
First published anonymously in 1828, this faux autobiography chronicles landmark events in Sassoon's childhood, such as his first riding lesson and a particularly important cricket match. Fox-hunting represents the young Sassoon's happy-go-lucky frame of mind in the years before the war broke out.

Lifting the Latch: A Life on the Land – Based on the Life of Mont Abbott of Enstone, Oxfordshire
Sheila Stewart
For nearly eighty years 'Old Mont' lived and worked on the land. This remarkable piece of social history – constructed from a series of taped conversations and illustrated with 17 specially commissioned aquatints – is an unsentimental portrayal of a lost way of life. ▶

If You Loved This ... (continued)

◄ Over the Hills and Far Away
Candida Lycett Green
John Betjeman's daughter's story of her
journeys round England on horseback
blends family reminiscence with a celebration
of the British countryside.

Human Voices
Penelope Fitzgerald
The 'human voices' of this enchanting
novel are those of the group of eccentric
broadcasters at the BBC during the air raids
of WWII. Listeners tuning in had no idea
what human follies and dramas were
unfolding behind the scene. Romantic,
ironic, tragic, this is based on Fitzgerald's
own experience.

The Land Girls
Angela Huth
A wonderful wartime saga set in the West
Country. Land girls Prue, Ag and Stella are
thrown together and, despite their very
different backgrounds, form a friendship that
will last a lifetime. In 1997 the book was
adapted for the screen, starring Anna Friel,
Catherine McCormack and Rachel Weisz. ∎